THIS
ATOM BOMB
IN ME

THIS ATOM BOMB IN ME

LINDSEY A. FREEMAN

 **REDWOOD PRESS** Stanford, California

Stanford University Press
Stanford, California

Printed in the United States of America on acid-free, archival-quality paper

Library of Congress Cataloging-in-Publication Data
Names: Freeman, Lindsey A., author.
Title: This atom bomb in me / Lindsey A. Freeman.
Description: Stanford, California : Redwood Press, 2019. | Includes bibliographical references.
Identifiers: LCCN 2018009274 |
ISBN 9781503606890 (pbk. : alk. paper) | ISBN 9781503607798 (epub)
Subjects: LCSH: Freeman, Lindsey A.—Anecdotes. | Oak Ridge (Tenn.)—Biography—Anecdotes. | Oak Ridge (Tenn.)—Social life and customs—Anecdotes. | Nuclear weapons industry—Tennessee—Oak Ridge—History—Anecdotes.
Classification: LCC F444.O3 F75 2019 | DDC 976.8/73—dc23
LC record available at https://lccn.loc.gov/2018009274

Cover design: Rob Ehle
Cover photos: (foreground) The author as a girl, in front of a playhouse built by her grandfather, Frank McLemore. (background) The "Baker" explosion, part of Operation Crossroads, a nuclear weapon test by the United States military at Bikini Atoll, Micronesia, on July 25, 1946. US Department of Defense, via Wikimedia Commons.
Text design: Bruce Lundquist
Typeset at Stanford University Press in 10/16 Sabon

For my mom, Bobbie J. Freeman

the effort to perceive simply the cruel radiance of what is

—James Agee

what's that gotta do with this atom bomb and me?

—Father John Misty

MY GRANDFATHER WAS AN ATOMIC COURIER. He drove secret materials for the first uranium-powered atomic bomb from the Manhattan Project city of Oak Ridge, Tennessee, to various locations across the country. He liked it well enough to keep driving through the Cold War for the Atomic Energy Commission (AEC). My grandmother was a bowling enthusiast and donut-making Cemesto homemaker. My mother and uncle went to high school in a red brick building adorned with a giant atomic symbol containing an acorn as its nucleus.

The atom-acorn assemblage is the totem of the town. Not only is it the ubiquitous symbol of atomic Appalachia,

but by linking the community together symbolically it also marks a shared culture and sweeps us up in its substance. For those of us in its orbit, its spinning is our spinning; its hard acorn body, always already full of future potential, is also our collective body, as we embody culture and place. The atom-acorn is a concentration of all the Oak Ridges that have happened, never happened, might happen, and are happening, combined with the ways in which we have made sense of these happenings.

I lived the first few months of my life directly under the atom-acorn totem in Oak Ridge, until my father got a job in a less interesting town in the northeast corner of the state, the finger-shaped part of Tennessee that pokes at Virginia and North Carolina. The place we went to had no secret atomic past and no national laboratory; no atoms with their jaunty capped acorns dotted the landscape. Instead, its claim to fame was a large chicken-processing factory in the center of town. During the first week after the move, my mother was driving my five-year-old brother around our new town. Zooming down the road cater corner to the chicken factory on a sweltering July day, my mother pulled behind a truck filled with birds headed to their beheading. She had the windows rolled down because the car didn't have air conditioning. Feathers were flying everywhere. My brother shouted, "It's snowing!" My mother cried for her loss, for her disappearance from atomic cosmopolitanism, and for her relocation to Morristown, and the regular, less atomic American landscape.

When I was young, I too felt disappointed, robbed of growing up in the science city for smart people, where the nuclear bourgeoisie rubbed shoulders with the future physicists of America, and where the Manhattan Project and the nuclear industries that followed created a new sensorium of everyday and extraordinary experiences. The connection between Oak Ridge and Hiroshima was the first big shock of my life. The facts are stark. Oak Ridge was a secret city engineered by the United States government for the sole purpose of creating fissionable materials for an atomic bomb. The site was chosen for its proximity to the Tennessee Valley Authority (TVA) dam in Norris, Tennessee, and its steady supply of electricity, as well as for its seclusion. During World War II, in this secret location tucked between two ridges, over seventy-five thousand people lived and labored for the war effort. Only a small fraction of workers knew what they were producing; the rest knew simply that they were working to support the Allied cause in the war. On August 6, 1945, most Oak Ridgers learned the true nature of their work from the radio, just like everyone else listening over the airwaves in other parts of the nation and across the world.

Oak Ridge National Laboratory, Oak Ridge, Tenn.

Oak Ridge has been a major nuclear science and security site since its beginning: first as an important node in the Manhattan Project, later as a key production location for the nation's Cold War arsenal, and now as a place not only for the production and maintenance of parts of nuclear weapons but also as a center for medical research, nuclear storage, national security, and the emergent nuclear heritage tourism industry.[1] The Oak Ridge National Laboratory (ORNL) and the Y-12 National Security Complex are still the major institutions of the city. These places are important, but the atomic sensorium is not contained in sites: it radiates throughout the city, goes underground, swims and dives through rivers and tributaries, and ignores boundaries and barriers of every stripe. I carry it in my own body. It is both outside and inside, material and immaterial, pulsing and still.

My atomic immersion began when I visited my grandparents as a child and encountered the vibrant matter of Oak Ridge.[2] As an adult, I write about the place to try to untangle its mysteries—feeling a magnetic pull and mnemonic push to do so. For me, Oak Ridge is not just a city but also an organizing system of thought, a structure of feeling, a place full of nostalgically charged objects, and a magic geography that I can't shake.[3] In *Empire of Signs*, Roland Barthes questions our ability to "contest our society" without challenging the limits of language in understanding our situatedness in the world, calling this practice "trying to destroy the wolf by lodging comfortably in its gullet."[4] To test these limits, Barthes writes about the Japan of his imagination—a place far removed from his culture and a site for decentering thought.

Here I follow a different path through the woods from Barthes in *Empire of Signs*. I write as an atomic exile about the spaces of my childhood. I put on my favorite red hoodie and climb deeper into the lupine maw, only to discover that the wolf has swallowed my grandmother, and even though she is not what she once was, I do not wish to destroy her. I want to understand this place that shaped her life, my mother's, and mine. I want to study how its aliveness and its history suffused my childhood. So I write carefully about atomic materiality and sensuality as it sticks in and irradiates my memory. I compose a sociology of what I came to sense and to feel about the place before I began trying to interpret it as a scholar by tracing spaces, objects, affects, and memories of the ordinary, the fantastic, and the atomic uncanny.[5] I examine how people, places, things, histories, and memories are entangled and enmeshed with each other, forming mnemonic assemblages that are good to think with.[6]

SOCIOLOGICAL POETRY

My methodology relies on imperfect data, even "woefully imperfect," as W. E. B. Du Bois writes in his essay "Sociology Hesitant"; my data "depends on hearsay, rumor and tradition, vague speculations, traveller's tales, legends and imperfect documents, the memory of memories and historic error."[7] Using this methodology and working with suspect data, I want to revive a peculiar genre—sociological poetry. "Sociological poetry" is the term C. Wright Mills used to describe James Agee's *Let Us Now Praise Famous*

Men and the style he tried to replicate in *Listen, Yankee*. Mills was deeply inspired by Agee's account of 1930s Alabama sharecroppers; he went so far as to describe the book as "one of the best pieces of 'participant observation'" he had ever read. Agee's writing gave Mills an example of a new way to think and do sociology. In an essay in the journal *politics*, he described sociological poetry further:

It is a style of experience and expression that reports social facts and at the same time reveals their human meanings. As a reading experience, it stands somewhere between the thick facts and thin meanings of the ordinary sociological monograph and those art forms which in their attempts at meaningful reach do away with the facts, which they consider as anyway merely an excuse for imaginative construction. If we tried to make up formal rules for sociological poetry, they would have to do with the ratio of meaning to fact, and maybe success would be a sociological poem which contains the full human meaning in statements of apparent fact.[8]

Mills was working toward something similar in his own writing. He was preoccupied with finding a methodology for sociology that would be a way of telling compelling stories with "full human meaning" that allowed for the inclusion of the author's personal feelings and emotional connections toward the objects of study. He wanted to show the vibrations of social worlds and to communicate the reverberations of those worlds as felt in the writer. Throughout his career, Mills tried to convey what he called the "tang and feel" of experience. In a letter to his parents,

Frances and Charles Grover Mills, dated December 21, 1939, he wrote: "From my mother I have gotten a sense of color and air. She showed me the tang and feel of a room properly appointed, and the drama about flowers."[9]

This is a lesson we could already have learned from Virginia Woolf's *Mrs. Dalloway*, where the drama begins with Clarissa Dalloway's announcement that she will "buy the flowers herself." And with this simple assertion of a task to be completed for a party, we are flung into the atmosphere of a social world. The problem for the sociologist is that this is a fictional world—it doesn't get us to sociological poetry but to a poetics that blooms with sociological knowledge. Instead of studying an actual person or group of persons, as we would in sociology, Woolf invents Mrs. Dalloway and her social network. Of course, Mrs. Dalloway and her world are not created in a vacuum but are constructed from Woolf's fictive *and* sociological imaginations. Woolf tosses us into an ocean of timespace already in motion, in which over the course of a day when the action of the novel takes place, we feel how each moment is suffused with anticipations, desires, dreads, and memories. In this way, my study of an atomic childhood at the tail end of the Cold War is like *Mrs. Dalloway*: it is an attempt to write how it feels to be caught up in something ongoing, like a surfer in a wave or like someone remembering. I'm trying to write how it feels to be tossed into towns, swept up in historical flows, and coasting along with or overwhelmed by culture.

I am also inspired by the ways in which sociology and poetry are coming together in the twenty-first century. I almost leapt out of my chair when I heard Fred Moten describe his method of "critical poetry" as "a mode of sociology that is in turn only achievable by way of and as an expression of an active experimental poetics." Moten is also thinking about Du Bois' essay "Sociology Hesitant," as well as his own suspect "data." Moten reverses Du Bois, even as he thinks with him, in order to create critical poetry, and a form of sociology, that hesitates, breathes, and takes the time it needs to get close.[10] This is the kind of writing that can capture what it feels like to be inside a sensorium.

Like Mills and Woolf, I too am working toward a way of writing that takes emotions, senses, colors, and microclimates seriously. And also like Mills, I am thinking with forms of knowledge passed down to me from my mother and grandmother, combined with my sociological training.[11] Like Moten, I am after a method of thinking and writing that tries to perform both the visible and invisible things that rule our lives. I reverse Barthes, as I think with him, in order to remember what it was like to sit inside the wolf's gullet with the atom bomb inside me. My hope is that this project leads to some understanding of an atomic Appalachian habitus born of nuclear spaces, southern living, Reagan-era politics, and the culture and cultural objects of the Cold War.[12] In addition, this experiment attempts to add texture to the thinking about the relationship between materiality and memory by bringing in the atomic as one example of the instability and vibrancy of matter in general, and to do so through vignettes that pile.

ATOMIC MEMORY

In *The Nervous System*, Mick Taussig likens the shape of the forebrain, which is thought to contain "civilized consciousness," to a "mushroom-shaped cloud" that hangs over the midbrain, the site of memory. That thought hangs over the words to follow, and as Donna Haraway reminds us, "it matters what thoughts think thoughts." [13]

WARNING

Cormac McCarthy writes in *The Road*: "Each memory recalled must do some violence to its origins. As in a party game. Say the word and pass it on. So be sparing. What you alter in the remembering has yet a reality, known or not." [14] McCarthy and I went to the same high school, twenty miles away from the Atomic City; I trust him and have attempted to heed his advice.

ATOMIC COMBRAY

A soft poetics of atomic summer rises from the bomb-shaped city. Oak Ridge was my Combray. I visited my grandparents in all seasons, but my atomic childhood features summer. This was when I could go and stay for a week because school was out; when I could swim in the gigantic swimming pool built by the Army Corps of Engineers for the atomic workers and their families, at first just for the white ones and then for everyone. For a while, it was the largest pool in the South. Every hot day and early evening it swallowed me, along with scores of other children I did not know and the occasional lap-swimming adult who sometimes knew my mother. It was in summer that I would run around the track while my grandmother walked, marking each lap with a stone, a remembrance for each ellipse. It was in summer that I would careen down the street on the bright-red skate-wheeled wagon that my grandfather made for me. These activities added up to a giddy triathlon that I was unaware I was training for.

CEMESTO "B"

For a long time I went to bed early in a lumpy twin bed in a bedroom of my grandparents' Cemesto "B" house. The little house sat on a street next to other little houses of similar design. They were part of a master plan, housing for the Manhattan Project. The houses were laid out at slightly different angles, as if you were a relatively neat person but happened to be playing Monopoly on a bumpy rug or shag carpeting. In this case, the uneven flooring was the contours

Residential Section of Oak Ridge, Tenn.   78276

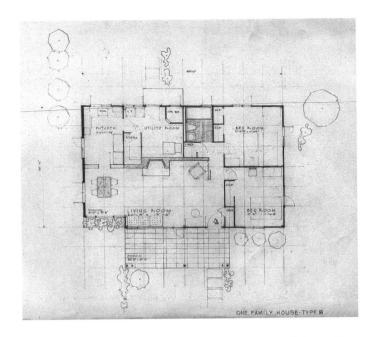

ONE FAMILY HOUSE-TYPE B

of the East Tennessee landscape, the ridges and the rolling hills. The point of this Monopoly game was not a quest for riches and real estate but rather for an atomic bomb.

The "B" denotes the house's place in the alphabetized scheme. The letters correspond to the size of the house and the number of bedrooms, "A" being the smallest and "E" the largest. The house was built from a material portmanteau—Cemesto—a composite building material made from cement and asbestos with a core of sugarcane fiber insulation, a filling the texture of cotton candy. Cemesto panels were placed horizontally into wooden frames of the house in order to create the walls. It was introduced in 1937 by the Celotex Company Corporation; a prototype appeared at the 1939 World's Fair in New York City. During World War II, the architectural firm Skidmore, Owings, and Merrill used the Cemesto design to make my grandparents' home and nearly three thousand others just like it. After the war and in the spirit of modernism, Cemesto became a favored material for architects interested in low-cost building materials. Frank Lloyd Wright and Charles and Ray Eames were among its newly won fans.

MONDRIAN

My atomic childhood is a Mondrian painting. On the ordered streets and in the uniform houses of the former secret city my grandfather's blue pickup truck fills a square, his blue jeans color in another, my grandmother's favorite outfits in red or yellow are folded neatly into others. Their yellow house has its own square, too.

REAGAN ON TV

Inside those squares could be found yet another square—the Magnavox square. Sometimes my grandfather and I would watch TV together while eating Planters Dry Roasted Peanuts out of their tall jar. He called them goobers. We would consume great big handfuls of them, causing our fingers to become dusty and salty. I thought they were a fancy snack because of Mr. Peanut's attire and monocle, a snack-sized yellow-legume cartoon version of Proust's Charles Swann. Our TV watching was much less aristocratic: *Hee-Haw* was among our favorite shows. Sometimes before our country variety program we would watch the news. This was a good time, unless Ronald Reagan punctured the small faux-wood-paneled square. If the president showed up, I knew our fun would be interrupted. My grandfather, a yellow dog Democrat, would become disgusted and say, "Hell, I can't even relax for one evening without seeing that idiot get on or off a plane waving like a monkey in a zoo." At these moments I felt relieved to have been born under Jimmy Carter, the peanut farmer president.

PLAYHOUSE

The women who passed by on the sidewalks of Oak Ridge were different from those I knew in Morristown, because they were Mondrians. Cars and trucks tucked into driveways, next to square houses, were also Mondrians. My playhouse made up of only horizontals and verticals, propped up on red-stained wooden planks, was also a Mondrian. I mondrianated in front of it wearing a boxy denim jumper with red buttons, a yellow t-shirt, and blonde hair.[15] The atomic factories on the other side of town were Mondrians, too; they complemented his later, more chaotic period of painting, the paintings he made in the early 1940s as an exile in New York City, the paintings that made up his own Manhattan Project.

COMPOSITION B

My mother, too, is a Mondrian—neat and severe in her Oak Rigidness. Her thin black slacks like De Stijl lines, her blonde hair filling a frame, a blue Oxford-cloth shirt tucked into another frame, and still another with her famous yellow pantsuit painted bright and square.[16]

DECANTATION

In Samuel Beckett's essay on Proust he writes, "The individual is the seat of a constant process of decantation, decantation from the vessel containing the fluid of future time, sluggish, pale and monochrome, to the vessel containing the fluid of past time, agitated and multicolored by the phenomena of its hours."[17] As Beckett notes, the past when viewed through the glass of nostalgia is rarely washed in dull tones; it is most often chromatically rich. The images of my atomic childhood in Oak Ridge are vividly rendered in primary colors, which are occasionally taken over by the glowing green that seems to always represent radioactivity. By contrast, my memories of Morristown surface in more muted hues: the cream color of dogwood blooms, the warm brownish rouge of red-clay bricks, and blues mixed with grays, like the shutters that cling to the homes of Colonial Williamsburg.

OVERDOSE

Once while visiting my grandparents, I became sick with a cold: a betrayal of the body in summertime. In winter this seems a logical physical condition, but in summer it feels like a twisted knot in the organization of the universe, throwing off the right order of things. Just as Marcel's grandmother gave him beer, champagne, or brandy for his asthma in *In Search of Lost Time*, my own grandmother, attempting to adjust the equilibrium of my small body, gave me children's Tylenol and put me to bed. Marcel and I both longed to play; for him it was in the Champs-Élysées, while for me it was the Elysian Fields of my grandparent's honeysuckle-lined backyard. Homer thought Elysium lay on the western edge of the earth by the stream of Ōkeanos; I knew it was in atomic Appalachia, not too far from the Tennessee River.

When my grandmother left the room, she absentmindedly left the bottle of orange-flavored chewable Tylenol on the nightstand. When I woke I felt much better, leading me to the obvious deduction: if a little bit of medicine made me feel a little better, surely the entire bottle would cure me immediately, basically lacing up my Nikes for me and sending me out to play.

This is not what happened.

MOONING THE RUSSIANS

When I was well, which was almost always, my brother and I would play a Cold War game we called "Mooning the Russians." It was vaguely related to the space race and the arms race but mostly had to do with showing the Reds our asses. The Ruskies, most certainly spies, would pass by my grandparents' house trying to seem nonchalant. Wearing t-shirts and driving American-made cars, just who did they think they were fooling? We would show them we knew what was up by dropping our Jams® in their direction. My older brother would order me and I would lower my shorts. We always said "for America!" Once, a carload of teenage Reds really seemed to enjoy the mooning. They orbited the yellow house in their cherry-red hotrod like a planet orbiting its sun, in predictable circles, anticipated trajectories. It wasn't until the third or fourth time that I realized they were the same spies, only on loop, so crafty were they in their espionage.

TALKING CAR

Along the back roads between Morristown and Oak Ridge, rural culture reflected itself into the cosmos. Sunlight bounced off old Airstream trailers and satellite dishes turned toward the sun with a hungry heliotropism greedy for channels. We traveled these roads on weekend afternoons in my dad's silver Nissan Maxima with the windows rolled down for the breeze. I sat in the backseat, hanging my arm out alongside the door, the car warm against my skin like something alive. My brother sat next to me listening to his Sony Walkman, reading a paperback.

No one said much on these drives, but occasionally the car would interrupt the silence to let us know that the "fuel level is low." Maxima had a gentle human voice. Prompted by her warning, we'd pull over for gas, my brother and I leaping out for Slurpees, as the car told our dad, "Key is in the ignition." When it was getting dark and everyone was tired from the day's adventures, Dad would drive us home. If he forgot, Maxima would remind him, "Lights are on" or "Parking break is on," which she oddly pronounced as "bocking break." It was 1985 and we had a talking car. It felt like the future.

When she said "Left door is open," I believed that

she was addressing me directly and that she cared for me. Maxima didn't wish for me to be flung out across the highway; she wanted me safe inside her vehicular body. If I was on the right side, I felt her protection even more. She had a slightly different way of saying "Right door is open" that sounded a bit more breathy, as well as more urgent. A tender bomb of feeling would well up inside me at the sound of her words of caution. She seemed more than a car.

Though I didn't know it at the time, our Maxima's voice was actually the result of a tiny phonograph. Her soft warnings were recorded on a three-inch, white plastic record cut with six parallel grooves, one for each phrase she said. When she was triggered by the device's control circuitry to alert us to something, a stylus would drop into the correct groove and her little record would play. When she got older, her voice began to fail; it became very quick and high pitched or very slow and deep at unexpected intervals. Her voice sounded strange, as if she were struggling to reach the right register but couldn't quite get there. The irony was that these exposures of the mechanical nature of her voice made Maxima seem more vulnerable and more human.

Eventually Maxima was replaced. Our new car lacked a comforting voice. I've never been in a car since then that spoke to me, that I felt cared for me. It turned out that talking cars were not the future—just another techno-utopian moment of my childhood. Maxima had been my DeLorean, driving me to the future, taking me back to where I came from. And then she was gone.

MISTER ROGERS' ARMS RACE

One fall when October's work was ending and it was time for cooler November, Mister Rogers took on the Cold War through a series of TV programs titled "Conflict."[18] In five episodes and five different colorful sweaters he explored the nuclear arms race through allegory in the Neighborhood of Make-Believe. In each episode we left Mister Rogers' Neighborhood and travelled by a magical red trolley to another world, where the puppet King Friday the Thirteenth was suspicious that the neighboring land of Southwood was building bombs. The king's hackles were raised when he discovered that Corney—a snaggletooth puppet, dressed in a bowtie and tuxedo, a carpenter and handyman—was making huge numbers of a mysterious part for Southwood. The king speculated that the small blue pyramids Corney was churning out could be used in weapons work. Spurred by this fear, the king's imagination quickly moved in a quantitative direction: if Southwood was building a million bombs, King Friday the Thirteenth's kingdom would have a million and one.

As the king's paranoia increased, it infected the kingdom: he began training civilians as generals, recruited folks to manufacture bombs, and cut funding to the arts. Meanwhile, young puppets in school discussed gas masks and air-raid shelters; a grown man dressed as a dog was a spy for the war; and a braille message, at first mistaken for a secret war missive, revealed that "that which is essential is invisible to the eye."[19]

In response to the increasingly tense climate, Lady Elaine

and Lady Aberlin began a peace movement composed of people and puppets. They set out to demonstrate the goodness of the residents of Southwood and to avoid the horrors of war. As "soldiers of peace," they took their mission to the neighboring land, where they discovered the residents were building a bridge with the pyramidical shapes, not bombs. With this revelation the mad game of speculation came to an end.

Mister Rogers was no stranger to addressing difficult topics; he had already taken on death, with a pentagon, and divorce, with a pretzel.[20] In the eighties, the nuclear arms race was another difficult fact of life that Fred Rogers handled in his soft but overtly political way. He closed the last episode in the "Conflict" series by saying, "I hope you'll talk with the grownups you love about how they feel about things like war and peace, being angry and loving; that way you'll be able to find out what the history of your family is, and all the many ways they've celebrated peace in their lives."[21] I suspect that many children who took his advice ended up in the same hard place I did, with a family history of Americans who found peace only through war—my Oak Ridge relatives, who when asked about peace return like a skip on a record to state: "It was a terrible thing, but we had to do it. Thank God we had the atom bomb and not the other guys."

DR. STRANGELOVE AND THE ANGEL OF HISTORY

There is a picture of me sitting astride the replica of *Little Boy* outside the American Museum of Science and Energy in Oak Ridge: I'm holding on with one hand, my other is in the air, and my mouth is slightly ajar. It looks like this is my first rodeo. I'm riding the faux bomb like Major Kong in *Dr. Strangelove*, facing the tail instead of the nose—my

back to the future. In front of me is the museum and the story of the bomb and its mushroom cloud, the story some call progress but others call madness.[22]

TIMESPACE

Each August, antinuclear activists in white hazmat suits gathered on the rolling hills of Oak Ridge to remember the atomic bombings of Hiroshima and Nagasaki, and to protest the city's ongoing weapons work. The summer sun reflecting off their suits gave them a powerful, magical radiance, as if the whiteness of the laboratory had been let loose to run wild. The first time I saw them, I thought they were astronauts practicing for space, but I came to understand that they were activists dreaming of time.

MISNOMER

The name of the city was a great disguise, a nom de guerre. Oak Ridge carried with it a feeling of wooded hills, of turning leaves—from yellow to bright red—elevated, and balanced on a precipice. It conjured a sensation of something of beauty hanging in the balance. From the name alone it was impossible to guess that the world's largest supply of fissionable uranium was kept there in the hubristically named Uranium Center of Excellence. Seeing the city's name on a map or hearing its soft vowels thud into harder consonants, one would hardly guess that this little sidewalked city of thirty thousand people held the key to America's nuclear stockpile, ready to go.

ATOMS AND ACORNS

Once my mother carried me all the way up to the Chimney Tops of the Great Smoky Mountains, my sneakers rhythmically smacking her haunches like soft spurs of canvas and rubber. At the summit we put on plaid flannels and ate granola dotted with carob. We looked across the tree-carpeted mountains to neighboring North Carolina. My mother pointed to where my grandfather was from. She told me about my great-grandmother, Ella McLemore, who died before I was born. She said that Ella was a mountain woman who gave her coffee as a child and didn't celebrate Christmas.

My mother said that when my great-grandmother was old, my grandparents tried to take her to Oak Ridge to live with them, but she found the city frightening. She called it "the city of lights." Ella didn't like how the factories glowed at night and how the streets were lined with sodium lamps illuminating the sidewalks and cars. She missed the pleasures of darkness in the cool folds of the mountains. So Ella went back to her little house in the holler, where for the rest of her life she foraged for acorns, roasting and eating them with wild huckleberries for sweetening. She didn't choose the life of the nuclear family like my grandparents; she wasn't born into Oak Rigidness like my mother and I were. She never wanted to live under the atom-acorn assemblage that was the totemic emblem of Oak Ridge. She didn't have a hard acorn at her core, forged overtime in the blinding light of whirling atomic energy—a light that could never be turned off. As I listened to my mother's story, I imagined Ella, on the other side of the mountains, on the other side of history.

As we hiked down the trail past the twisting laurel and hearty rhododendron, Ella was forgotten.

LIGHTNING BUGS

During civil twilight on warm August evenings, I set to work collecting lightning bugs in a jar. The labs in Oak Ridge would pay you for a Mason full of them—scientific research, they said. As my grandparents lounged, I flitted around their yard, chasing the red and black flying beetles with their magical glowing ends. This was my duty as an atomic citizen.

GLO WORM

My grandmother gave me a Glo Worm toy she found at a carport sale. I remember playing with it in the yard under a carpet of crimson leaves and running it over the ridges of the golden corduroy couch in the living room. I remember its soft, plush body encased in pea-green pajamas, and its deep blue eyes and satisfied smile set into a hard head topped with a nightcap, tipped in orange. I remember pressing  the mechanism that kicked on the light and reveling in my small, radiant victories.

My grandmother remembered how I tied my toy to her town; how deep in play and working at insect ventriloquism, I would have the Glo Worm say: "I'm from Oak Ridge, I glow in the dark."

Glo Worms were not radioactive; tucked inside their nightclothes were battery-powered switches that turned on a light, so that when the torso was squeezed in the right spot, its plastic head would glow, mimicking bioluminescence. I was too young to understand the mechanics of the toy and the ways insects sometimes glowed in nature. Yet somehow I knew that things in Oak Ridge were likely to glow; I had a vague sense of nuclear power. I had already begun to absorb the myths of atomic Appalachia, and I spoke them back, loyal as a dummy.

TOPSY TURVY

When I was young, I had a Topsy-Turvy doll representing three fairy-tale characters in unsettling simultaneousness: Little Red Riding Hood, her grandmother, and the wolf. Little Red Riding Hood made up one half of the doll and a wolf-grandmother assemblage made up the other. They were connected at the waist, their torsos nightmarishly fused. In a feat of deceptive drapery, the skirt of Little Red Riding Hood obscured the wolf-grandmother half, while the skirt of the wolf-grandmother covered up Little Red Riding Hood. Little Red Riding Hood's skirt was solid red, the color of coxcomb. The wolf-grandmother wore a floral dress with small red flowers on black cloth, like remembrance poppies bursting through a field of nothing. The wolf-grandmother's outfit was topped by a bonnet trimmed with a halo of lace. To bring the wolf or the grandmother

into play you would move the bonnet to cover either the wolf face or the grandmother face. The trouble was, after you moved the bonnet or lifted up the skirt for the first time, you knew what was under the skirt and on the other side of the bonnet. There was no way to forget this knowledge, "in many ways . . . a terrible lesson; in many ways a magnificent one."[23] This was a lesson in how tightly history, biography, cultural imaginaries, and social worlds are sewn together.

It was nearly impossible to engage only one character at a time, not only because of the knowledge of the human-beastly attachment but also because of the materiality of the doll itself. Parts of the hidden others were constantly emerging during play: the triangle of Little Red's hood would jut out from under the wolf-grandmother's skirt; a wolf whisker would stick out of the grandmother's bonnet; threads of the grandmother's light-colored curly hair would remind me that behind the wolf visage was a human face. It disturbed me that no matter which way the doll was flipped, the hands remained the same: small, pink nubbins with nothing to suggest a wolf. This seemed to give contrary evidence to what I had been told, pointing toward human consumption of the animal instead of the opposite.

Before I was given the doll, I already knew the story of the beast gobbling up the grandmother, the folly of youth, and the dangers of the forest, but the doll introduced new corporeal possibilities, new angles to the fairy tale that reading and hearing the story did not encourage me to think about. With the doll it was always already too late for moralizing: the three characters existed as one and needed each other for their ongoing existence. No one was inside the belly of another; there was no possibility of a queer birth, no violent cesarean section like the one depicted in the Grimm Brothers' telling splitting one from the other two. If the conjoined characters had had cloth organs, they would have been shared: cotton lungs would have drawn cotton oxygen; a cotton heart would have pumped cotton blood through the singular doll body that comprised them all. In my small, pink hands they were all one beast, and I could decide which face to show the world.

NO RED

"Commie." The word spins her out like a top. She becomes a thin fury in a newsboy cap whirling through a grubby men's bathroom, fighting hard with small fists to defend her dad against the slur. Later she talks with her father about the fight and asks him if he is a communist. Agitated, he replies: "I'm no red. I just fight for what I believe in." This is how the film *The Journey of Natty Gann* begins, how I met one of my childhood heroes, and how I learned again the power of red.

ATOMIC SCOUTS

I joined the Brownies, the junior version of the Girl Scouts, because of a photograph I saw in the Oak Ridge Children's Museum that irradiated my desire to be part of a gang of girls—a troop. The black-and-white snap, taken in 1951

by Oak Ridge's official Manhattan Project photographer, Ed Westcott, showed young atomic citizens decked out in smart uniforms—berets, kerchiefs, buttons, patches, and belts—proud emblems and accessories of the bold, new American generation. Many wore the black-and-white oxfords that my mother called Mickey Mouse shoes.

In 1963, the Boy Scouts of America issued their Atomic Energy merit badge; a patch with a red-and-blue atom stitched into a background the color of yellowcake.[24] An equivalent badge was never issued for the Girl Scouts. No matter. The scouts of Oak Ridge hardly needed this patch. Their uniforms were already sewn with their town's very own atom and its accompanying acorn. And what's more, they lived and breathed atomic energy. They marched past the atomic factories just as they would walk past the local drugstore or ball field. For them, it was regular, everyday.

Since my scouting affiliation was based in another town, I was never able to march with my compatriots past factories born for the Manhattan Project. Instead, I was taught how to sew a potholder that looked like an enormous grape. When I learned the new scout leader was the mother of a girl I did not like much—the two wore matching sweater sets in the pale, shimmery colors found inside oysters—I dropped out. Instead, I prowled around alone, a composite of Davy Crockett, Nancy Drew, and Natty Gann sporting a faux raccoon cap, worn brown corduroys, and a small, red backpack where I kept my compass and mystery novels written by Carolyn Keene. Never able to live up to the image that inspired me, I lost interest in scouting and grew more intrigued with nuclear spaces and spies.

DRESSER DRAWERS

I found treasures among my grandparents' things, especially in their dresser drawers. Inside the brass-knobbed compartments rested a tangle of bright-yellow Juicy Fruit chewing-gum wrappers with their spiked, silver astronaut underlayers reduced to crumples; old buttons that could be repurposed as wheels on a miniature of Thor's chariot, like those Walter Benjamin found in his mother's sewing box;[25] costume jewelry in garish colors utilized in one of my favorite games called "jewel thief"; and stray documents of the atomic past that I sometimes borrowed, wedging them as bookmarks into the Nancy Drew mysteries I hoped would make me a better atomic detective. It was in those drawers that I found snapshots of my grandfather leaning nonchalantly against the white unmarked GMC truck he would drive in the service of the AEC, wadded-up pale-blue pay stubs destined for deposit at the Y-12 credit union, and other official-looking government missives. These important documents were not neatly organized but scattered throughout the drawer's rectangular space, nudging the buttons and wrappers, kissing the old photographs bent at the edges and creased at odd angles like scars that have healed but retain a physical reminder of having done so.

"Memory, as I have tried to prove, is not the faculty for classifying recollections in a drawer, or writing them down in a register. Neither register nor drawer exists," wrote Henri Bergson.[26] The compartments of my grandparents' dressers opened up a world for me, and I would never talk about drawers "disdainfully," as Bergson does. Still,

I know he is right: drawers and their magical contents are not memory, and they are not a metaphor for how memory works; rather, they are sites of possibility for the irradiation of memories.[27]

ATOMIQUE *PNEUMATIQUE*

At the Y-12 Federal Credit Union, named after the Y-12 National Security Complex, secret messages pass through pneumatic tubes. I ride there with my grandmother in her enormous gold Chevy Nova on secret missions. We pull up to the designated spot. Magical communiqués made up of complicated formulas calculating hours worked, values assessed, pay measured by the clock, the market, the Geiger counter, are sucked up, zipped over, mulled over, and responded to. Returning messages are equally mysterious—green rectangles bearing the faces of presidents, pyramids, and numbers. On a good day a lollipop tags along to sweeten the deal. The tubes of the credit union resemble the old *petit bleu pneumatique* system in Paris, now defunct, the little blue messages piling up forever in the corner of the dead-letter office.

SPACE SHUTTLE CHALLENGER

The day after my eighth birthday, Christa McAuliffe and six astronauts set off on the "Ultimate Field Trip." All morning, it seemed as if they might not go. It had been exceptionally cold in Florida; surfers had taken to wearing thicker wet suits; citrus fruits were freezing in the groves;

and there were icicles on the launching pad at the Kennedy Space Center. When NASA finally made the decision to go ahead, we assembled in tight little knots of anticipation on the floor of the classroom as our teacher set up the live CNN broadcast. The countdown from Launch Control activated my nervous system in increments of T-minus.

Liftoff temporarily cured my anxiety, my ache for departure. We were all jubilant for a moment, as we watched the severe beauty of Challenger soaring in the air. My teacher wolf-whistled through her fingers as no child could. And then, in a giant explosion of colors, it was over. A plume of smoke twisted toward the stratosphere, like a soft screw burrowing into the sky. I didn't see the seven fall into the Atlantic, only the moment of the explosion, the turn of the smoke screw breaking off in two directions,

skywriting the letter *Y* and a backwards question mark. Then the live feed cut away from the sky to the ocean. I felt a sense of unreality, a detachment from time and place. The world seemed suffused in various blues as an image of a ghostly parachute with jellyfish movements drifted into the frame.

There was a terrible stillness in the classroom as we absorbed the truth that the space-teacher and six astronauts were gone. The emotional architecture of the room crumbled: some of us cried, some sat stunned, someone couldn't stop saying "No, no, no, no, no . . ." We had all dreamed of space, of weightlessness, of wearing space suits emblazoned with the futuristic-wormy logo of NASA.

We were allowed to go home from school early. My mother came and got me. At night we watched the news and listened to President Reagan like he was a good guy. He addressed a whole country of Americans, unprepared for failure. His speech was elegiac; he spoke poetically of the astronauts and promised we would never forget how they looked as they prepared for their mission and waved good-bye in their powder-blue space suits, just before they "slipped the surly bonds of Earth to touch the face of God."[28]

I couldn't sleep that night. I had a head full of exploding shuttles and astronaut ghosts. I tried to think of Neil Armstrong, Buzz Aldrin, and dreamy Sally Ride shooting safely into space, but I couldn't quite get there. My mind was caught in a loop, focused on the terrible brightness of the accident, where life was extinguished at great speed and dropped into the sea, without a beginning or an end.

LOOK HOMEWARD,
ATOMIC ANGEL OF HISTORY

I found *Captain Atom* in the enchanted world of the Oak Ridge Public Library. He was resting atop a bookcase under a stained-glass window adorned with the atomic symbol. This made him seem doubly magic. I brought him down to the floor, where I read cross-legged, bathed in a slash of sunlight sprinkled with color from the window. Reading a comic book from the beginning of the Atomic Age in the Atomic City had a disorienting effect on me; I felt as if Oak Ridge was a place to tease time.

Like the city where I found him, Captain Atom's atomic origin began in secret:

There were no witnesses except the giant telescopes on earth . . . The space explosion of the atomic warhead was awesome! At the instant of fission, Captain Adam was not flesh, bone and blood at all . . . The desiccated molecular skeleton was intact but a change never known to man, had taken place! Nothing . . . absolutely nothing . . . was left to mark the existence of what had once been a huge missile! Nor was there a trace of the man inside!"[29]

Before he was Captain Atom, he had been Allen Adam, a scientist, tucked in an aluminum rocket, a modern casing three times lighter than steel. When the atomic bomb inside the rocket exploded, Allen Adam and the spacecraft were completely disintegrated. As he drifted in the post-explosion liminal space between human and superhuman, in a swirl of atoms and radioactivity, Allen Adam might have been thinking something like what Thomas Wolfe, the Proust of Asheville, wrote in his famous novel, *Look Homeward, Angel*:

I am . . . a part of all that I have touched and that has touched me, which, having for me no existence save that which I gave to it, became other than itself by being mixed with what I was, and is now still otherwise, having fused with what I now am, which is itself a culmination of what I have been becoming. Why here? Why there? Why now? Why then?"[30]

In that moment, timespace had been obliterated, and all that the scientist Allen Adam had been was blown apart. Both the future and the past seemed equally uncertain.

Then something fantastic happened. As he floated in the ether, he found that the essence of his human brain remained. He set to work. Atom by atom he reassembled his body. He returned to Earth, a radioactive fallen angel, a superhero decked out in the primary colors of a Mondrian painting. He was now Captain Atom, a comic-book dream, a new angel of history for a new age. Unlike Benjamin's angel of history, as he was flung into space, the scientist looked away from Earth; he turned his back on the ever-piling disasters of humanity and set his sights on the future. But the disasters—culminating in a mushroom cloud—reached him in his rocket and the continuum of history was exploded. All the events of the past were flung across space, not yet fallout but spread out and invisible to the Americans, who watched below through their powerful telescopes.

In this fantasy, the new angel who returns to Earth is allowed to stay, in order to "awaken the dead, and make whole what has been smashed."[31] Captain Atom lived luminously. He dreamed of peace with the Soviets, he battled evil with his atomic powers, but he didn't realize that he had become part of the emergency, dressed up as progress, "half echo of the past, half menace of the future."[32]

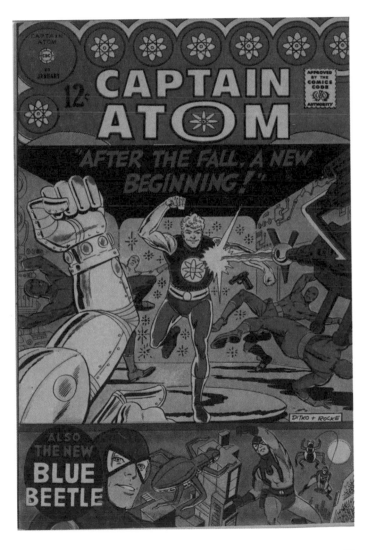

CAPTAIN ATOM'S SUIT

The first time I saw Captain Atom, I might have swooned. He had great legs and a flair for dressing. He was a super-dandy. When he went critical, his hair turned a silvery-white blond. He wore candy-apple red tights and royal-blue boots that reached midcalf. His chest was marked with a bright-yellow circle containing an atomic symbol radiating action lines in every direction. Under his skin he wore a suit of liquid metal, which according to the comic books protected those around him from his toxic super-body that radiated radiation. The suit was a gift from President Eisenhower.

Captain Atom was an example of the new humanity that peopled the atomic sensorium created in the wake of Hiroshima. He was a successor to Max Weber's vision of early twentieth-century folks enclosed in their iron cages and steel casings. In *The Protestant Ethic and the Spirit of Capitalism*, Weber, with a melancholic tone, notes that the material world of commodities and irrational rationalism had wrapped around people with a tightness previously unknown. It had changed them. The new casings, fabricated since the summer of 1945, were not like the iron traps or steel skins that Weber imagined; they were now inside us, no longer an outside layer but another layer before the muscle and the fat, liquid metal, fast like mercury, powerful and toxic, and nearly impossible to shed. When Weber was writing at the turn of the twentieth century, it was already too late to toss the cloak of the material world off our shoulders with ease. By Captain Atom's time, we had entered a new sensorium. The cloak was now irradiated, and we absorbed it into us; no longer something light or heavy that lies upon us, the cloak *is* us. Captain Atom's suit is yet another example of how the atomic—fantastically, terribly—re-enchanted the world.

GLOWING ROWERS

On Melton Lake, a couple of miles from my grandparents' house, rowers kitted out in tight spandex suits of every color glide past Canadian geese that have never heard of radiation. Melton Lake not only plays host to visiting crews but also houses its own—the Atomic Rowing Team. Their symbol is a circle with the fan shape inside that warns of radiation. I loved seeing the Atomic Rowers train, bodies and muscles working in unison as they sat in their long, sleek, ruby-colored boat, dipping their lemon-yellow oars in the lake. I stood on the shore rapt, watching as they slid the radioactive symbol in the water, drawing it out, dipping it in, drawing it out, dipping it in, drawing it out . . .

RADIO FLYER

Douglas Lake was my Lethe, my water of oblivion. Into its muddy, liquid mouth I plunged again and again with my grandmother and a Radio Flyer. We would start at the top of the hill next to the basketball hoop with its droopy, rotten net jutting out from a pine tree, where we played Around the World and Horse and where my grandmother nearly always won. She would climb into the wagon first and scoot to the back so she could hold on to me. She'd let her legs hang outside, her muscled calves ending in dirty

Keds working as brakes. Once I was inside, Nan would let out a whoop and with a sudden start we were off, propelled into a heightened sensorium of thick pine and mud-scented wind, the metal rub of the wagon, the polyester scrub of my grandmother's culottes, and the clanking and crunching of the wheels over the wild yard. The speed was unimaginable. The bumps were always thrilling and unexpected; we never bothered to clear branches and rocks from our route.

There was always something a little wild and reckless about my grandmother. She would "steer" us into the water, but topography and gravity were doing most of the work. The ride would end in the final rush of the cool wet and the heavy pull of the water grabbing at our chariot. Quickly, we would pull our dripping ride up along the shore and back up the hill to do it all over again. We were Sisyphuses for our pleasure.[33]

LADY COCKS

My grandmother kept a yellowed article about her high school basketball team in her bedside table. It was a nostalgia piece about the glory days of Cocke County basketball in the late 1930s and early 1940s. This is how I found out why she was so good at shooting hoops. The article, from her hometown newspaper, the *Newport Plain Talk*, featured a photograph of ten lean countrywomen, with my grandmother in the back row standing ramrod straight with her arms bent severely. She looked like she meant business. In cursive script moving in a loose diagonal from her head, my grandmother wrote: "I look mad. Because we lost."

Accompanying the article was a poem penned by Ben Shaver on Valentine's Day, 1940. The poem paid tribute to the Lady Cocks from Cocke County High, celebrating their beauty and hoops prowess even while documenting a heartbreaking defeat:

When the CCH girls filed out to report,
A more beautiful sight was never on court.
Their stream-lined figures and flashing smiles,
Seemed to spell victory all the while.

They shot their goals in sight and out,
And looked superior without a doubt.
And when the end of the quarter came,
The game belonged to the dashing dames.

And not until the game was well under way.
Did their grip on the score begin to sway.
But when the last two minutes rolled around,
We wanted to stop every clock in town.

For the girls came back with a six-point sweep,
That took all Newport right off their feet.
But time wouldn't wait in her mighty flight,
And caused them to lose a hard fought fight.

Then to the invaders of our town,
They gladly handed the golden crown.
We may lose the title on the ball and hoop.
But we'll sure lead the way on real good looks.

The winning team was lead by Wilma Jackson, standing 6′3″. From the photograph, my grandmother appears to be the tallest on her team; she was 5′8″.

The loss broke a string of championships for Cocke County High; it also marked the end of my grandmother's basketball days. This was the last time she wore her scarlet satin uniform and the last time she heard fans shout "Go Coward!," calling her by her maiden name. It was the end of being part of a team of strong, rural women performing for crowds.

After that season, she graduated, married my grandfather, become a McLemore, and moved to the secret city of Oak Ridge. When the article appeared decades later, the reporter wrote, "Her whereabouts are unknown now." My grandmother got a kick out of that; she thought it made her seem mysterious.

There is a popular idea that World War II gave women a chance to do physical work and play ball, but in many rural places women were already doing these things and being celebrated for them. In fact, my grandmother used to tell a story about meeting an army officer in charge of assigning soldiers to war placements. When he found out she was the very same Nan from the famous Lady Cocks, the officer changed the location of where my grandfather was sent to fight and sent him to someplace less dangerous than he was originally assigned. My grandfather said this likely saved his life.

RECURRING DREAM

One summer when I was visiting my grandparents, I had a recurring dream, every night for a solid week. It was a nightmare where radioactive monsters were out to destroy the world. The monsters had once been regular people, but they had undergone a nuclear metamorphosis after eating radioactive fish pulled from Melton Lake. They were transformed into hideous beings, shuffling, zombie-like creatures. One-by-one everyone in town was killed or made monstrous. My brother and I would be the only ones left, our parents the penultimate pair. The monsters would back us up to the black walnut tree at the edge of the yard, and I would wake up with a start, my heart pounding out of my chest like a cartoon. In the repetitive oneiric sequence, the only thing that would change was the color of the Volkswagen Beetle parked across the street from the final scene. Most often it was painted antique white, like Herbie the Love Bug (but without the racing stripes), other times it was the color of lemon yogurt; once the car had the hue of a blueberry, like the VW my dad had when he was young and wooing my mother.

THE GHOST OF HOMECOMING

Although my parents had long been divorced, my grandmother found it unseemly to display pictures of my mother—even when she was young, years before she met my father—with other men. So when I would visit, I would see photographs of my mom on the tops of mantles framed in golden rectangles locking arms with dates obscured by Wite-Out. Anyone visiting my grandparents' home might have thought my mother had a thing for phantoms. Sometimes no one could remember who the date was under the glob of white. While on one level I found this hilarious, on another it disturbed me, this erasing of my mother's past with correction fluid.

There was something about the whiteness itself I hated. I came to understand why Mondrian's white squares took more effort than his brightly colored ones, why more brush strokes were applied. He wasn't laying a background or creating a blank space for future possibilities; the white marked the end for those spaces—they would be white and nothing else. My grandmother's efforts with the tiny Wite-Out brush did something similar: my mother would only have my father and no one else. There is something in this insistence that the past is past (or maybe never happened at all) that causes me consternation, much more so than if it had simply been left alone, as a record. I learned from Toni Morrison that "invisible things are not necessarily not-there."[34] If my mother's dates had remained in living color, if they had appeared casually above the fireplace dressed in early sixties fashions, they wouldn't have troubled me so much as their exaggerated absences did.

THE GHOST OF WHEAT

On a crisp autumn day, after much begging and pleading, my grandfather drove me to a place where some folks had seen Oak Ridge's most famous phantom, the Ghost of Wheat. The ghost is named after one of the farming communities that was confiscated, evacuated, and eviscerated to make room for the Manhattan Project in the early 1940s.[35] He is thought to be the spirit of a farmer whose land was forcibly taken by the government, but nobody really knows for sure. Sometimes the ghost has appeared dressed in overalls and a worn plaid shirt, and occasionally he has manifested as a penumbra of light or balls of fire.

The road we took to get to the phantom's supposed stomping grounds was maintained by the Department of Energy (DOE); a sign warned: "Only Authorized Vehicles Allowed." When he felt we were close enough, my grandfather eased along the shoulder and parked the truck close to the little white George Jones Memorial Baptist Church. The church was the only original Wheat building still standing—a persistent whiteness against the innocence of trees.[36]

Sitting there by the side of the road, I had the feeling we had not only driven across town but across time and into the pre-atomic past, and in a way we had. We listened to Barbara Mandrell and George Jones as we waited: "I Was Country When Country Wasn't Cool" filled the sonic space of the cab. It took me years to realize my grandfather was having fun with me when he chose that particular cassette. I remember how he rifled around for it and how the sounds of the tape cases crunching against each other set me on edge: it sounded like stepping on crickets. Later I learned that the church had been named for an entirely different George Jones, a preacher who had donated money and land to the Wheat community. The church was too old to be named for the country-music singer George Jones, known for his womanizing and hard drinking. Those two Joneses were simply what the Dutch call *naamgenoot*, people who share the same name, but have no other connections.

In those days my patience was short, so it didn't take long before I saw something. I looked anxiously over at my grandfather, and in his square glasses I saw an oblong white shape: THE GHOST! Then I turned to look straight ahead where I hoped to see the Ghost of Wheat not simply as a reflection in my grandfather's glasses but in all his glory. What I saw instead was the headlight of a motorcycle. The Ghost of Wheat is part of my nervous system, as well as the nervous system of Oak Ridge, unruly, a bit paranoid, sometimes matter, sometimes spirit.[37]

ASA JACKSON'S FABULOUS
PERPETUAL MOTION MACHINE

At the Museum of Appalachia, twenty-five miles from Oak Ridge in Norris, Tennessee, there is an idle perpetual motion machine. Asa Jackson, a farmer gifted with mechanical skills, designed the apparatus in the mid-1800s. Featuring a six-foot-tall wheel and seemingly thousands of handmade wooden parts—gears upon gears—painstakingly carved and fitted, the machine was said to have spun without stopping. The invention was designed for the practical activity of threshing, but it had a greater effect on the imagination. It promised boundless energy free from effort—energy that was too cheap to measure.

During the Civil War, Jackson kept his invention hidden in Black Cat Cave near Murfreesboro to keep it safe from the Yankees. As the legend goes, whenever he had to leave his invention for any length of time, he would remove key pieces, bringing the machine to a halt. In 1870,

Jackson died, some say with the missing key pieces in his pocket. After his death, the machine was stored in a shed, where over the years it was snacked on by rats and time.

I first encountered Jackson's ingenious invention in the late twentieth century, while on a school field trip to the museum. A melancholy feeling settled over me when I read the panel explaining that the knowledge of how to make the wheels spin was lost to history. Jackson's machine was simultaneously a provocation from the past and a glimpse of a future that never arrived—a future-primitive vision of threshing without end.

Later on I imagined Jackson's host and the Ghost of Wheat together on a long walk. In my fantasy, the Ghost of Wheat was trying to explain to Jackson's ghost how the TVA created Norris, a new dreamtown containing a hydroelectric dam that would supply seemingly endless renewable energy. He went on to explain how the dreamtown would eventually contain the Museum of Appalachia, which would try to represent the ways of life that were now as ghostly as the two phantom farmers. The Ghost of Wheat outlined the history of the region, how thousands of people had to move to make Norris and its dam possible, and how people had to move again when the government built Oak Ridge right next door. Jackson's ghost felt how this history hurt, how it smarted, but he also understood the logic of TVA and Oak Ridge—how the latter's efforts to separate isotopes of uranium used the same separating logic of the thresher, and how when you have machines like this, you must take care to hide them from your enemies. I imagined that the whole interaction left the Ghost of Wheat feeling loosened and separated from his fellow phantom, alone in his resistance to what others call progress.

TENNIS COURTS, PLAYERS

A tennis court means nothing by itself, or at least very little. It is an abstraction. It means something only when people move inside its grids, when they write another poetic court on top of the clear lines drawn by the rules of the game.

In Oak Ridge, I played on city courts below rickety, rectangular apartment buildings—former dormitories built for the Manhattan Project. During World War II, Oak Ridgers danced on these courts every weekend, cutting imaginary rugs over the gridded lines where scores were kept: love, fifteen, thirty, forty, game. Each Saturday night, the loveliest among them would be singled out and a new "Tennis Court Queen" would be crowned.[38]

When I played tennis in Oak Ridge, it was toward the end of the Cold War. Sometimes serious-looking nuclear physicists, or people who I imagined were nuclear physicists, played doubles on courts next to me. I knew they knew more about speed and angles than I ever would. I liked to steal glances at them when I went to fetch the balls that had collected in the net. I wanted to know their secrets. Other times groups of women would arrive at the courts for league play. They would file down the hill in accordion-pleated skirts or phantom-white tennis dresses falling midthigh, each wearing charming socks adorned with brightly colored balls bobbing at the base of their heels. I would study them clandestinely between forehands, backhands, and overhead lobs, picking out my own Tennis Court Queen.

In Morristown, I took tennis lessons from Peggy Howell on her dairy farm. The red concrete court with its crisp white lines sat out in a field maybe half an acre from the farmhouse. In the summer, knots of blue bachelor's buttons and deep yellow dandelions filled holes in the chainlink fence; in the fall burnt-red and dusty-yellow leaves huddled there. As we drove down Howell Road to the farm, humid bursts of beastly smells filled the car. Peggy joked that it was "country without the club." After my lesson, my mother would be waiting to pick me up at the blue edge of dusk, her slender form leaning against the old, rusty BMW with the curved smile of a plastic visor resting on her head.

SPACE DOGS

Sometimes I would bring my dog, Pepper, occasionally known as Dr. Pepper, with me to Oak Ridge. Pepper was a black-and-white mutt with a lot of spirit. My grandparents loved him, and he seemed to enjoy his atomic vacations. He lolled in the shade of the carport and chased the fluorescent-yellow tennis ball through the tiny tongues of fresh-cut grass, his too-big red collar flapping against his chin. My grandfather built him a dog house with real shingles and trim. It looked like a typical American home but not like an Oak Ridge home: it had no place in the alphabetized arrangement; it was not a Cemesto.

On one visit my grandfather told me a troubling story: the Soviets sent a dog into space and she died. Her name was Laika (in Russian the name means "barker"). She was chosen by Russian scientists to be flung into space on the basis of her calm demeanor: she was able to stay in very small spaces for long stretches of time, able to tolerate extreme vibrations, willing to subsist on a special gel diet, and adept at handling gravitational forces. She was also selected for her good looks and charisma; she famously delighted reporters by barking into a microphone after they asked her questions. Good-natured to the end, she barked upon liftoff but did not survive Sputnik 2's journey. Still, Laika was considered a national hero and a martyr for communism. There is a memorial to her in Star City, outside of Moscow; postage stamps; and even a brand of cigarettes carrying her image. Pepper resembled her.[39]

My grandfather told me the worst part was that all along they knew she would not return to Earth. At the time the Soviets only knew how to send spacecraft into the cosmos but not how to get them back safely. I was both repelled and fascinated by this story; I couldn't help thinking of Pepper in space, wondering about his chances out there. I thought about the time he hurt his hind leg and had to wear a clear plastic cone over his head—he looked then like a space dog—and how when he slept he sometimes barked as if he was in another atmosphere. I used to think he was dreaming that he was under water, but maybe it was space he was dreaming.

PRIPYAT, THE CITY OF ATOMS AND ROSES

On April 26, 1986, there was a nuclear meltdown at the Chernobyl Nuclear Power Plant. An experiment had gone awry in Reactor No. 4. Nearly nine tons of radioactive material was thrown into the air, creating a black plume of radioactive smoke that smothered the city of Pripyat. The entire city was evacuated. It was hard to wrap my head around the fact that a city could be there one day and all its inhabitants gone the next. It was even more frightening because this was a nuclear city full of experts—scientists and engineers—and something had gone horribly wrong.

Pripyat was an "atomograd," a monocity—a Soviet city dedicated to a single industry; its sole purpose was to steward atomic energy for the USSR. Pripyat was located just three kilometers from the Chernobyl Nuclear Power Plant, making an easy commute for the nuclear workers who lived there. It had been designed as a model city, promising a beautiful, orderly, and prosperous Soviet future. Roses were planted everywhere. The flowers decorated the city in pink jumps. The citizens loved them so much they never picked them (it was also forbidden by the state). A rose features prominently on the city's coat of arms, resting on an enormous atomic symbol like a boutonniere. The dandy atom and its flower hover over a tiny hammer and sickle that appears to be struggling to hold them up (it's hard not to think of this as foreshadowing).

At school, at home, and on the news, the adults of America tried to assure everyone that this was a Soviet mistake. Their science was no match for our science; their safety standards were below our safety standards; their infrastructure was weak, crumbling. Some folks who still remembered Three Mile Island grumbled, exercising the nervous system of atomic America. There was a lot of talk about managed risk in order to avoid a meltdown.

I learned from living in atomic Appalachia that science is only supposed to touch *us* when it's good. In light of the Chernobyl disaster this sentiment was hard for me to square. Pripyat was killed by nuclear science and became a ghost town. Reactor No. 4 was entombed in a sarcophagus made of concrete and steel. The planned amusement park, set to open on May Day, would never see visitors; the impressive Ferris wheel with its bright yellow cars would never spin the Soviet citizenry and its youth in a circular orbit. Its Palace of Culture Energetik was stuck in an endless torpor. The post office floor was littered with letters never delivered. The convenient trains were damned to rust on the rails awaiting passengers that would never come.

Still, not everything was static; a strange afterlife continued in the city's ruins. The liquidators charged with cleaning up after the disaster swam in the once majestic Azure Swimming Pool. The Wormwood Forest circling the city new in greenery worked to adapt to its radioactive reality, while enormous catfish circled in the failed reactor's cooling ponds, and wolves steadily killed the pets left behind and the feral dogs that were their offspring.

After the Chernobyl accident, the USSR built another city on a similar model to Pripyat in order to house the people who had been evacuated. The new city, Slavutych, was an inexact clone. It looked similar, but recent history had killed its chance for sameness. Slavutych's residents loved it, but primarily because it reminded them of Pripyat.

THE LOST SEA

At first, it was like stepping into an aquarium world: there were soft sounds of water moving slowly, and the lighting was low and strange. The rocky walls were covered with spikey anthodites, known to poetic spelunkers as cave flowers. Once inside, we became privy to the lie in the advertising: the Lost Sea of Sweetwater, Tennessee, is actually a lake inside a cave. The appeal to the sea was meant as a hook to lure tourists off the interstate—salty water sounds more exotic to the landlocked.

To my delight we drifted through the cavern in a glass-bottomed boat. The air that rose from the water was cool, and the boat's drifting created an alternative air conditioner. The transparent surface beneath my feet revealed schools of very white, nearly translucent, rainbowless rainbow trout. They looked ghostly. My grandfather said it was from the absence of sunlight. The guide added that they lacked the predators found in nearby lakes. "They've been hiding here for a long time," he said.

The longer I spent in the cave, the more it began to feel like a museum of natural and unnatural history. In the Pleistocene Era, long before it was a tourist attraction, the Lost Sea was home to enormous jaguars (a skeletal specimen from the cave now rests in the American Museum of Natural History in Manhattan). The cavern system that holds the Lost Sea has also served as a hideout for Cherokee people, Confederate soldiers, and Prohibition-era bootleggers. The Lost Sea even contained a speakeasy known as the Cavern Tavern, where customers could imbibe cave-themed cocktails alongside the United States' largest non-subglacial underground lake.

In the 1960s, folks thought that the Lost Sea might be a good place to hide out from nuclear war. Sweetwater's proximity to Oak Ridge had made the local citizens extra nervous. In response to a growing fear of nuclear attack, members of the local Civil Defense unit filled the caves with provisions—enough food to feed twenty thousand people for several months. When I visited in the late 1980s, the subterranean space still held the memory of its fallout-shelter days: rusted canisters of certainly stale saltines and large

drums of water were piled alongside and below the stalag-
mites and stalactites that had never heard of nuclear war.
To experience the Lost Sea is to experience what Foucault
calls a "heterotopia," a type of set-aside space containing
multiple spaces and times that can be felt all at once.[40]
Only part of this history is nuclear, only part of this history is lost.

SUMMER KNOWLEDGE
(AFTER DELMORE SCHWARTZ)

Lacustrine scenes feature prominently in my summer
memories. Proximity to murky waters and their devoted
communities taught me many things. I grew to understand
that swimming in lakes takes a confidence not required
for pool swimming. I learned that water moccasins liked
hanging out in the trees that grew out of the shallow
areas near the muddy shores and that copperheads loved
the cool patches under my grandparents' lake house. My
grandmother told me that my grandfather would chop off
their heads with an axe to protect us, transforming the
brutal act into a tender gesture. I imagined their serpen-
tine skulls falling into a pile like pennies in a jar, buying us
a secure future.

I learned that my brother wasn't allowed to ride his bike
to the trailer-park community down the long gravel road
because "stuff goes on there." What kind of stuff was unimaginable to me then. I learned that Mary Lou next door
was a "good neighbor" and that the "stuff that goes on" at
her house was okay to take part in.

I discovered that people came to the lake to drink beer and that if I hunted around the rocks, I could find brightly colored caps that smelled sour and metallic for my bottle cap collection. I learned that if you stomped on the golden mushrooms that grew by the mailbox you could create a dusty, mustard-colored cloud, but if you ate them you could die.

I found out that if I forgot my bathing suit, we could get a new one at the camp store down the hill, but that I'd have to wear a two-piece instead of the swim team–style one-piece Speedo I preferred: I've always felt vulnerable with my soft belly in the sun. Wrapped up in a terry-cloth towel, quiet and shy in my new swimsuit, I learned from overhearing my grandfather tell my grandmother that the bikini swimsuit was named after an island place obliterated by a megaton nuclear bomb.[41] "You just wouldn't believe the stuff that goes on," he said. That summer I learned that I still had much to learn about the stuff that goes on.

EXPECTING THE WORST, NOT GETTING IT

One Oak Ridge summer day, I tossed open the screen door to an unexpected scene. In the grass, I saw a furry hump, twitching. The living mass was emitting sounds, little high-pitched cries that seemed almost human. At first I thought it was the neighbor's dog and that he had been injured. Slowly, and with great effort, the animal revealed herself: a fawn just born. As she tried to raise herself up, her legs, thin as bread sticks, crumpled, and she fell in a heap. Tendons, muscles, and ligaments shaking, she tried again.

Again, her spindly legs went akimbo and she was horizontal, flat as a cartoon. The movements were so awkward and the collapsing so total that I thought something was horribly wrong. Images from TV specials about Chernobyl featuring grotesque animals, born with multiple heads, mismatched limbs, and internal organs on the outside of their bodies, popped into my head. These visions combined with the stories and rumors I had heard about wildlife in Oak Ridge, genetic codes hacked by radiation.

My fears swelled and I stood transfixed. My mouth tasted like copper. The fawn's mother retreated into the trees when she sensed I was there. The fawn made shrill sounds as her mother stepped out of view. My dog was making low whines. I detected a shared but unequal sense of desperation—from the deer, from my dog, and from me. The atmosphere felt charged with three mammalian nervous systems expecting the worst.

After some time the tiny deer managed to get her back legs up and leaned onto her front ones; she was bent at the joints, an animal kind of kneeling. More twitching, more great effort, and she was on all four hooves. Surprised, she waggled her tail, and the small white spots on her back shimmered like sequins. Not gracefully but not altogether awkwardly, she disappeared into the small wooded area bordering the turnpike at the edge of my grandparents' yard. She went where her mother had gone.

I remained for a while watching the trees, prolonging the spectacle I had just witnessed of a beautiful creature on the not-yet-brown grass of summer becoming what she was supposed to become.

CARL PERKINS

One afternoon while riding around in my grandfather's blue pickup truck listening to cassette tapes, I became no more than a set of ears, a beating heart, and a whirling mind anxiously following the words of Carl Perkins' song "Tennessee":

Let's give old Tennessee credit for music
As they play it up in Nashville everyday
Let's give old Tennessee credit for music
As they play it in that old hillbilly way

.   .   .   .

They make bombs they say, that can blow up our world, dear
Well a country boy like me, I will agree
But if all you folks out there can remember
They made the first atomic bomb in Tennessee

As the song faded and I gazed out the passenger's side window, the city I saw all around me was the same Oak Ridge it had been just minutes ago, but as the tape ribbon wound around the spools, the city's contours and even its name became overwhelming. It was a haunting moment, "when familiar words and things transmute into the most sinister of weapons and meanings."[42]

Like the Manhattan Project days when Oak Ridge was absent from commercial maps, Perkins avoided naming the city in his song. In his rendering of nuclear history, the bombs come simply from Tennessee. To me this avoidance made the city more powerful, a secret once again. As "Honey Don't" carried us to the end of side A, I knew this place could destroy the world and that I was riding shotgun with the "they."

KATY'S KITCHEN

A mysterious blue barn with an odd concrete silo at its hip sat tucked into the woods, not too far from ORNL. Throughout the Cold War, the barn bore a series of strange names—Building 9214, Installation Dog, and Katy's Kitchen.[43] The last moniker was the one that stuck, the one I heard when I was a kid. It was named after Katherine Odom, an AEC secretary who enjoyed eating her lunch in the tranquil setting. But this place was far more than a pleasant spot to eat a sandwich: the barn-silo complex was rustic camouflage for a high-tech nuclear storage space.

Behind the barn's swinging doors was the entrance to a reinforced bunker dug into the hilly landscape. There was a long tunnel, deep enough for a tractor-trailer to be driven inside and completely hidden. At the end of the tunnel was a locked room, like a bank vault, which could only be opened with a secret combination. This room, enclosed behind heavy steel doors and surrounded by layers of reinforced concrete and steel rods, was the bunker within the bunker. At the core of all these layers of deceit, steel, and concrete, the AEC kept their secret deposits—highly enriched uranium from the Y-12 and K-25 nuclear plants.

Like the barn, the silo was another architectural lie: it was a security tower with a machine-gun nest manned by two guards on high alert twenty-four hours a day. The base of the silo was made of steel-reinforced-concrete pipes that were cunningly covered over with weathered wooden strips and rusty metal bands to make the building look authentic. Around the circumference of the area, power lines were hidden in the forest. The lines were strung between the trees, the branches providing cover, making it impossible for airplanes flying overhead to make out anything unusual. Alarms were tucked in the foliage along the forest floor, to alert security to would-be spies. Crepuscular creatures were constantly setting them off, exercising the guards and keeping them anxious.

By the time I was born, Katy's Kitchen was an unintentional monument to the Cold War—the false barn no longer held fissionable uranium, the silo had stopped wearing its wooden disguise, and the armed men had long ago vacated their perch for other posts, or more likely, retirement. Still, the hidden potential of the terrible material swarmed and nested in my imagination like the wasps that had taken over the silo. Katy's Kitchen activated my nervous system; I learned to question every barn, every seemingly benign structure dotting atomic Appalachia.

I was haunted by the knowledge that enormous trucks containing dangerous materials could be completely hidden away, like worms burrowed into the earth. I thought about my grandfather and his work as an atomic courier, wheeling the nondescript white semi-trailer truck full of who-knows-what for the government. I wondered if he ever drove into this secret tunnel in the Oak Ridge hillside when he trucked for the AEC; if he made jokes about having lunch at Katy's Kitchen; if he knew the combination to this particular vault of Cold War secrets; and if this crazy collage of rural-scientific-security architecture became part of his nervous system, too.

THROWN TOGETHER (AFTER KATIE STEWART)

Oak Ridge gathers itself together inside concrete laboratory buildings in lush, green valleys. The city spins itself together inside the glowing, Cherenkov-blue radioactive pools, where millions of billions of neutrons are produced in a second, making heavy isotopes for the creation of elements such as californium, curium, and plutonium. Oak Ridge keeps itself together by crafting elements to propel nuclear bombs, cause and cure cancers, and spin satellites and shuttles deep into outer space. The city brings itself together in secret, spinning a delicate balance between explosion and implosion—fission and fusion—through a mysterious substance called FOGBANK. Oak Ridge hurls itself together in public in its museum with its story of atomic prophecy, wartime secrecy, and patriotic sacrifice. The city steels itself together with its little atoms and acorns affixed to laboratories, high schools, and pawnshops, like the rivets in denim that reinforce areas of high tension. Oak Ridge throws itself together in the whirl of the atom and the acorn, like Mondrian dancing with Peggy Guggenheim, like a wolf circling before sleep.[44]

SCHOOLS OF MY MATERNAL LINE

My grandmother's high school sat in a garnet ring of twenty-seven red maples. One tree was planted for each Cocke County casualty in World War I. Each tree wore a placard at its base, like a dog tag, bearing the name of a soldier who had been killed. Every autumn the maples blazed red with remembrance. My grandmother told me that when no one was looking she talked to the dead men from the past, the trees-revenants, standing in for human forms.

Seventy-two miles away and twenty years apart, my mother studied under the sign of the swirling atom and its diligent acorn. In Oak Ridge, remembrance was replaced by selective amnesia. The specters of war were pushed to the edges of town, where sylvan laboratories, built along pre-atomic graveyards dotted with crosses and stones, prepared for more war. My mother didn't talk to men from the past; the landscape of her youth discouraged haunted chatter. After graduation, she carried Oak Ridge's spirit of forgetfulness with her. She sauntered into her college orientation at East Tennessee State University and said, "I'm from Oak Ridge, the Atomic City, and my atom's never been split."

SPLITTING

In 1974 in suburban Englewood, New Jersey, the artist Gordon Matta-Clark stripped to the waist and sawed a house in half. The work was called *Splitting*. It was an example of "anarchitecture," an art movement that played on and with anarchy and architecture. Sometimes I think

of my childhood home as having been split this way, the
red-brick colonial where I lived in Morristown and the yellow Cemesto where I stayed when visiting Oak Ridge making up two parts of the same domicile that held me since I
was born—the seams sewn together by my memory doing
battle against the sawteeth of forgetting.

FRUIT BOMBS

My childhood home sat nested inside the soft architecture
of landscape design. Dogwoods with milky flowers lined
the driveway, while a row of strong maples flanked the
front of the house like sentinels. Bright-yellow forsythias
bloomed along the fence at the edge of the yard. Tender
buttons of periwinkle bobbed in gentle beds, as the box-
woods slowly grew together. Ivy was kept in neat rows

lining the walk to the front door but crawled wildly up the house, latching on with woody brown tentacles, appearing to make one solid wall of its eastern side. On the western side of the yard, there was a magnolia tree, with large, waxy leaves and heavy blooms that sagged after a hard rain. On the northern side of the yard was a sweet-gum tree that shed piles of spiky fruit, called sticker balls, or sometimes goblin bombs. At the southern end, where the grass met the driveway, stood two large concrete pine-apples from Colonial Williamsburg, painted a warm gray. It wasn't until my brother toppled one over with the car that I realized they had the same body type as *Little Boy*.

STRANGE HARVEST

In my youth, the grounds of ORNL were thick with deer. The whitetails loved the fields of the nuclear reservation because they were protected from predators, plus the decades-old radioactive waste that occasionally surfaced tasted like a salt lick. Under these conditions, the deer population grew exponentially, and the animals began to trouble the nearby roadways. They collided with cars, smashed windows, took out side mirrors, and died messily across hoods.

To address the problem, the DOE invited deer hunters onto the normally restricted area for three weekends each fall to thin the herd. They timed the hunts to be at the height of rut, the mating season, so that the animals would be especially active and made more vulnerable by their love pursuits. The hunters assembled at dawn near the old Tower Shielding Reactor Facility site. They dressed in clothing printed like the forest, with a swath of blaze orange above the waist. Until dusk they traversed the territory around Haw Ridge and Cooper Ridge, where Oak Ridge scientists once dreamed of nuclear-powered airplanes.[45] The hills were made fragrant as hunters peppered the air with bullets, followed by the metallic tang of spilled blood.

I couldn't understand why the organizers of the hunt called it a harvest. No one in my family hunted. Each summer my mother talked to the dappled fawns that visited our yard. I remember a particular set of twins and her affection for the pair—she called them Flora and Fawna. Our knowledge of the hunts was secondhand: we read the reports in the newspaper and heard them on the local television news. We watched the footage of deer bodies gone slack, watched as some were carried over hunters' shoulders and others were dragged down the hill by their hooves to the radiation check station.

Inside the station wildlife personnel and Oak Ridge scientists used a bone saw to hack off a bit of each deer's foreleg, while the hunters slit dead animal bodies down the center, pulled out blood-dark livers, and placed them in Ziploc bags, which they then passed, wobbling like Jell-O, to officials in DOE jackets. Inevitably there was a joke made about the lack of BUCK jackets. The attempt at humor did nothing to slow down the officials, busy with their testing. The carcasses were scanned from tip to tail with an alpha scintillation device and a Geiger counter. Then beta scintillation detectors were used on the bone samples. Finally, sodium iodide detectors were applied to the livers to read gamma energies. The tests were looking especially for strontium-90 (found in the bones) and cesium-137 (found concentrated in the muscle). During every hunt there were deer determined to be too "hot" to be taken off the nuclear reservation, too radioactive to be turned into venison, and too toxic for taxidermy.[46]

CIVIL DEFENSE

As a child, I took it upon myself to exact the half-life of oblivion from everything I encountered. Each birthday, I asked for a bright-yellow, Civil Defense–style Geiger counter to help me in this task. Each birthday, I was denied. As a consolation prize, my grandmother bought me two banana-hued pencil dosimeters at a yard sale. They bore the iconic insignia of the Civil Defense: a bold blue circle holding a white triangle with a C and D in rounded, scarlet script. She explained that they were not actually pencils— you couldn't write with them. The designation had to do with their shape, slender and tall, and made to fit in your pocket. I was delighted with my dosimeters and carried them with me everywhere, imagining all the radiation they were soaking up. Every so often I held them to my ear, like a seashell, and listened. I drew them close to my Sony Sports Walkman, yellow on yellow, like a goldfinch on a forsythia bush. I pretended my Walkman was not a cassette tape player but a Geiger counter, a machine that could detect histories of radiation played in reverse. Without a proper Geiger counter I could never really hear the telltale sign of radiation detection—like mechanical beetles bouncing off each other in a tall jar—but I realized that silence is a kind of ticking, too.

NUCLEAR AUTUMN IN OAK RIDGE

All the autumns of my youth, we played soccer by a sweet little creek that was so gentle we never thought to ask if the water was laced with strontium-90 or toxic mercury, by-products of the city's nuclear industries. When the ball rolled out of bounds into the cool, shallow water, we'd scoop it up, take it under our polyester jerseys, and rub it along the fabric and against our bellies in order to get a good grip for the throw-in. Back in play, we'd trap the still-moist ball on our chests, thighs, and the tops of our feet, as if it were almost part of our bones, or better yet, we'd flick it off our heads for the forwards to run onto, quick as silver.

SPECIAL LUMBERJACKS

Meanwhile, across town, special lumberjacks in hazmat suits chopped down trees that made Geiger counters sing. Every fall the DOE checked each tree on the nuclear reservation, running their machines along the bark, against the grain of history, finally reaching the leaves. They were looking for evidence of phytoextraction—the process by which trees pull contaminants from the soil and push them into their leaves. The contaminated trees did not live to explode into fall color. They were cut into pieces and buried before their leaves had a chance to blow off the nuclear reservation and scuttle across town. Their arboreal lives were cut short, as their radioactive half-lives lived on beneath the soil, adding to the nuclear-zombie ecology, making up the Oak Ridge below Oak Ridge.

SQUARES OF TIME AS A PROTECTION AGAINST OBLIVION, PART 1

After my grandfather's funeral, my grandmother slid down the grid of the white-painted brick wall of her kitchen in front of a room packed with relatives, friends, churchgoers, and government employees—mainly my grandfather's trucker pals. Angular and dressed in black, she resembled the jangly line on a stock market crash chart. My grandmother had always been dramatic. It was not the bold gesture that affected me so deeply but the way it didn't seem "put on" the way her attention-grabbing antics usually did. This was real grief, raw and devastating. It was terrifying, more terrifying than seeing my grandfather, waxy in his casket, even more frightening than witnessing him lowered slowly into a dark rectangle of dirt. In my grandmother's collapse I saw her future death, and it scared me. At that moment my atomic childhood split, and I understood that life was made up of periods of brightness and darkness— there were moments when you could see the grid of your life clearly, and moments when nothing made sense. I set to work collecting squares of time, forming them into blocks of text, as a protection against oblivion.

THE LUPINE UNCANNY

As an adult, I had a dream I was in the yard of my childhood home in Morristown. I was wearing a red woolen hat, and snow was covering the ground. The world felt impossibly white. Then, suddenly, wolves surrounded me. The leader of the pack was large and gray.[47] There were also five or six smaller red wolves; their fur looked almost blonde. I was afraid of the larger wolf but felt close to the smaller, red ones—almost one of them. I made snowballs for each of the wolves and for myself, and we ate them. The gray wolf said, "We are eating history." I tried to say memory, not as a statement or counterargument but as a question. My mouth couldn't form the word. It was too full of snow, or numbed from the cold, or I was afraid, or maybe it was that this was a dream and simply lacked waking logic.

SOME TIME ALONE

One afternoon at Jennifer's house we learned all the words to R.E.M.'s "It's the End of the World as We Know It (And I Feel Fine)." In a fit of dystopian euphoria, we'd play the tape, pause, rewind, go back to the note pad, scribble out, and rewrite, making sure we got it right. We were trying to catch the words as they came along, thick and fast. The tape case with the lyrics had been lost. We were on a mission to fill in our knowledge and solve the mystery of this frenetic song with its melancholic undertow.

It felt like the end of the world, in a tan-carpeted bedroom on a brown tendril of land sitting between the highway and the woods in a small town in Tennessee. We were two young American girls jumping around a room, drinking screwdrivers, and shouting about the end times at the close of the Cold War. Later we climbed onto the roof with the tape player, using a large garbage can as a makeshift ladder. On top of the house and tipsy with vodka and our transgressions, we sang at the drivers speeding by: "That's great it starts with an earthquake, birds and snakes, and aeroplanes . . ."

The next day I sat alone in my Pepto-Bismol-pink room and listened again to R.E.M.'s manic song about the destruction of the world, reliving my adventure. This time different phrases took on more meaning. The refrain "It's time I had some time alone" caused me to experience a flood of feelings, a weird cocktail of bliss and dread. The music sparked a longing for companionship and the taste of citrus, alcohol, and wildness. I was stuck at home on a Sunday morning in Morristown, imagining the apocalypse from a white wicker chair in a red-brick house looking out onto a cul-de-sac anchored by a cherry tree.

SQUARES OF TIME AS A PROTECTION AGAINST OBLIVION, PART 2

My grandfather's death from heart failure created a series of black boxes blotting out some of the primary colors of my childhood. In mourning this loss, Oak Ridge's colorful grid of order and harmony took on darker shades. Like Ad Reinhardt's black paintings, my grandfather's sudden absence produced squares of time composed of layer upon layer of memory and forgetting. His death made some versions of the past and the future almost impossible to discern and imagine. Aspects of my grandfather's life, not yet conceived as mysterious, moved into the shadows, as possible trajectories of my own life followed suit. In each person we know lies a version of ourselves; when we lose someone, a part of ourselves is frozen at the age of loss. Proust referred to this as the "successive deaths" we all face throughout our lifetimes.[48] He experienced this as a painful but inevitable part of being human. A childhood version of myself—cut to the quick before middle school, the one who knew my grandfather—is part author of this text; other, later selves fill in the writing.

WAFFLE HOUSE, CHRISTMAS

For several years in a row, my grandmother, my mother, and I went to the Waffle House on Christmas. It was a tender ritual, aided by the softness of the waffles and the conflicting feelings of the season. We went partially because of absences in our family due to death, divorce, and drug addiction—a litany stolen from a sad country ballad. Our feelings of loss and disappointment met their sonic mismatch in the camp country songs spilling out of the jukebox speakers: "It's going to be another Waffle House Christmas / On the jukebox they'll be playing Christmas songs / I'll have a waffle and just pretend nothing's wrong."[49] The Waffle House stood on Illinois Avenue as an example of southern modernism, with its clear, crisp, yellow-and-black sign and simple, elegant design.

Located a few doors down from Atomic Pawn and close to the American Museum of Science and Energy, the Waffle House served atomic citizens from all walks of life and class backgrounds. Still, there was something a bit off, not quite right, about being there on Christmas, if you had any sort of Christian attachments or pretentions. For me, going to the Waffle House on the holiday felt subversive, maybe a little punk. Plus I loved waffles.

The interior of the restaurant was orderly and sparse. Orbs of light hung from the ceiling like dollops of creamy butter. A small, plastic, too-green Christmas tree with empty boxes wrapped up as if they were presents sat in a corner like a dunce. The place was always busy, so we had to dodge other customers as we made our way to a table. We would bypass the counter, where people eating alone usually sat, and climb into a plastic booth always already sticky with syrup. There we sliced up our golden grids. Our orders were always the same: my mother and I had pecan waffles, while my grandmother stuck with the classic, simple and unadorned. If we sat by the window, my mother wouldn't take off her sunglasses. Sipping her Lipton tea with lemon, she looked like Joan Didion, an observer, comfortable yet out of place.

While I ate, I made observations about the cooks, waitresses, and our fellow patrons. I worked like a naïve ethnographer as I cut my breakfast along horizontal and vertical lines. I followed the dictum of the Waffle House: "The people are the movie. The waffles are the popcorn." The holiday meal hung on a kind of innocence and its corruption. As we left, the odor of waffles mingled with the cold air in our hair and coats, becoming a part of our Christmas past, invisible monuments from distant winters.

WAFFLE HOUSE ADDENDUM

Thomas Forkner, a co-founder of the Waffle House chain, worked as a counterintelligence agent for the U.S. government during the Manhattan Project. Like my grandfather, he helped transfer sensitive material key to the development of the atomic bombs from Oak Ridge to Los Alamos. The trip between the two project sites took fifty-three hours of driving without stopping, with two men per truck and two men in a trailing car. They avoided driving through cities. I wonder if on those long rides in a trailing car following a truck full of secrets, Forkner dreamed of waffles and a pleasant place to eat them, a griddled oasis in the American landscape brimming over with butter and maple syrup.

AGNES MARTIN #1

In winter, Oak Ridge was an Agnes Martin painting, more subtle than a Mondrian. The city sidewalks formed grids in shades of white and gray, stripes of cool warmth laid out before the mountains. On the fog-smoothed surfaces of the city everything seemed to hang or skid along with less effort than at other times of year. But "it was not just the weather outside that had changed . . . Inside me there was a change of age, the replacement of one person by another."[50] Each chilly winter I turned a year older and chipped away at the ice block of my youth, revealing an older self, waiting underneath.

ATOMIC MARY AND THE ATOMIC UNCANNY

On cold winter mornings delicate hues blanketed the Atomic City. The placid blue of the empty swimming pool against the dusty pinks and light blues of the sky formed lines of effervescent color. I admired these lines as I walked, traversing the city at a brisk clip. I stopped only to perform my clandestine ritual at the oracle of the unthinkable—the Atomic Mary statue on the grounds of St. Mary's Catholic

Church. I kneeled down before her to slip off my gloves so that I could touch the rounded, white marble base where she stood. I traced the atomic symbol by her feet with my index finger. I fantasized that my action might bring her to life and that she would glow. The glowing would be brilliant, radioactive, and it would touch me. I, too, would become radiant.

Each time I practiced my ritual, I thought I could see Mary begin to move, her gentle marble smile widening; each time I didn't stay to see what would happen next. I felt blood singing in my ears and adrenaline flooding my legs. My body felt buoyed, chemical, liquid, and made to run. . . . Off I would go on quick sneakers over frost-crunched grass, unable to stop until I reached my grandmother's house, panting, my heart in my throat, feeling the enormous beating radiance of my life.

THE GLOW

Oak Ridge had a kind of weak phosphorescence at night, most maddening in spring when the leaves began to fill in the negative space between the branches, making it harder to see long distances. I tried to observe it from atop a narrow twin bed by peering through the blinds of my bedroom, but from my perch I couldn't see much: branches sweeping the air, the neighboring "B" houses, infrequent bats, and the occasional rabbit. I imagined a view to the atomic factories. There I knew was a glowing, humming mass vibrating against the deep denim blue of the sky and the smoky purples of the mountains.

THE SUMMER OF ICARUS

All through the summer of 1989 in the Mondrian town, I wore my Matisse t-shirt printed with *The Fall of Icarus*. Against my pale skin was the even paler Icarus: his body flung into space, his flame-red heart lit up against a gash of black, surrounded by bombs exploding into yellow stars. *The Fall of Icarus* was one of Matisse's cutouts, part of the series of artworks he made when he could no longer paint, when he was weakened from his bouts with colon cancer and his eyesight was failing. To create the cutouts the artist's assistants would paint large swaths of paper in colorful hues and hang them in neat grids on the wall to be selected by Matisse. Then he would scissor out organic shapes—fronds, coral, apples, horses, human bodies, stars—and pin them into his desired configuration. He called the practice "painting with scissors."

Matisse created the *The Fall of Icarus* in 1943 in Nazi-occupied France. As the artist wielded his tailor's shears, the sounds of Wehrmacht boots filled the streets, Allied artillery shells exploded in his garden, and Nazis occupied the very building where he lived. I had no idea of this collision of art history and World War II history as I selected this t-shirt again and again to wear on my atomic vacation. The brightness of the image blotted out all the history that was behind it, and I saw only the beautiful falling Icarus, a shape with a curious name.

In the Greek myth, Icarus' wings, made of feathers and wax, were melted from flying too close to the sun. Icarus had been warned about this very thing, but he couldn't resist seeing just how high he could fly. In this moment it is not

hard to imagine Icarus thinking like Oppenheimer: "When you see something that is technically sweet, you go ahead and do it and you argue about what to do about it only after you have had your technical success."[51] Icarus, like Oppenheimer, dreamed of technical success; he dreamed the gadget he was attached to would take him to new heights.

ATOMIC DOLLY

My grandmother loved making up skits and doing impersonations. She dressed up as Jesus, Minnie Pearl, Johnny Cash, and Elvis, but she was most famous for her atomic Dolly Parton act. She performed once a month at the retirement home a half mile from her house. I once watched her from a bedroom window as she was getting ready to drive off in her big, golden Chevy Nova dressed as Dolly. She was having a devil of a time getting her seatbelt over the enormous balloons she had tucked into her red-checked gingham blouse. One burst and I saw her chest become massively uneven. She pulled out the shriveled balloon and set it on the dashboard, a candy-colored loss. Not to be deterred, she reached into her purse and found a backup; she blew into it, and a bright-red replacement came to life. Still, the whole operation seemed precarious, like a tumbleweed on a treadmill.

When she got herself resituated, her chest looked like makeshift, do-it-yourself air bags. (DIY air bags did seem like something my grandmother would have made.) As she turned on the ignition, the tall, blonde wig flopped awkwardly on her head. She readjusted the cardboard guitar that sat on the seat next to her, using it to anchor sheets of paper scribbled with lyrics to the songs she planned to sing. I liked this private moment watching my grandmother, who didn't know she was being watched. A great wave of satisfaction washed over me when I realized that I, alone, was seeing the best part of her act. The nursing home folks would undoubtedly be entertained, but I had seen something not only hilarious but miraculous: the balloons remained intact, and off she drove.

I imagined her taking the improvised stage twenty minutes later with her repertoire of Dolly songs, but with adapted lyrics geared toward the people living at the retirement community. I knew her set because she had practiced it for me the night before. Some lyrics spoke to the concerns of older Americans everywhere, such as health insurance costs, pacemakers, and memory loss—for example, "PMS Blues" was reworked to "hip replacement blues." Other adaptations were Oak Ridge specific; they referenced the original Manhattan Project-era nuclear-processing plants (X-10, Y-12, K-25), the DOE, and glowing in the dark. She always closed with "9 to 5," which she turned into a ditty about uranium-235: "Working uranium-235, what a way to make a living." She'd shout over the typewriter sounds at the beginning: "Imagine that's a Geiger counter clicking, y'all!"

THE JOY OF PAINTING NUCLEAR WINTER

When I watched *The Joy of Painting*, I fell into a hallucinatory, chromophilic space of attentive distraction. I never painted along, never picked up a brush or prepared a canvas; I watched in order to lose myself in the soft, slow world of color and craft conjured by Bob Ross. His permed hair and gentle voice were hypnotic. My friends and I delighted in using his catch phrases: "Let's get crazy" and "No mistakes, just happy accidents." We applied his dictums to our lives, mockingly at first, but over time the words took on an earnestness we didn't expect. Bob Ross had a way of getting inside us.

Then one day he painted a mushroom cloud, only to quickly cover it over with a winter scene.[52] Was this a way of getting crazy? A mistake? A happy accident? A subliminal message delivered by a former Air Force master sergeant turned mild-mannered hobby painter? The episode started with the list of the necessary paint colors for the lesson marching across the screen in all capital letters: TITANIUM WHITE, PHTHALO BLUE, DARK SIENNA, VAN DYKE BROWN, CADMIUM YELLOW, YELLOW

OCHRE, INDIAN YELLOW, BRIGHT RED. The chromatic names invited the imagination to travel to faraway places and dwell in dreamworlds of color.

Aristotle and Plato conceived of color as a kind of drug, a *pharmakon*. Walter Benjamin thought that children were particularly sensitive to color and that when they engaged with their books, boundaries between themselves and the colorful texts dissolved—they found themselves inside the pictures. In *Chromophobia*, David Batchelor describes color as "a loss of consciousness, a kind of blindness," that can result in a temporary "loss of focus or identity, of self."[53] But color can also spark a moment of self-recognition, encourage a gaze, or elicit new attention. Color is orienting and disorienting by turns.

The show when Bob Ross painted the mushroom cloud began like so many others. He greeted the viewers and laid out the plan: "Today, I thought we'd do a fantastic little winter scene I thought you'd enjoy."[54] Bob Ross approached the canvas "covered with a nice thin layer of liquid white, all slick and ready to go." The brushwork started, and the slow motion of his hand and voice created a kind of soft machine of color and form. "Let's make a beautiful warm little sky up here, just using a bit of yellow. A lot of time winter scenes can be so cold that they are almost distracting. So, I thought today we'd make one that's very warm and very pleasant. I'm going to get a little red. It's very strong and will get your whole world on fire in just a heartbeat. Red's a very warm color. It makes you feel good."

My heart was on high alert. Ross had painted the shape of an enormous yellow mushroom cloud and began garnishing it with red, adding depth and menace. My twentieth-century nightmare began to emerge in warm, oily hues. The canvas became a threshold between the atomic unconscious and a winter afternoon at the end of the Cold War. I thought of my friend Melissa, who was convinced she could detect the color of people's auras. She diagnosed my aura as yellow: a canary-colored rhyme with Bob Ross' creation. That other great theorist of aura and color, Walter Benjamin, wrote: "Pure color is the medium of fantasy, a home in the clouds for the . . . child."[55]

Bob Ross continued: "Now let's come in very gently, very gently, let's just rub in a happy little cloud. See this dark area here? Don't kill it. That's your friend. It's alright if people look at you like you're a little strange. You tell them we gave you permission. You need those dark areas in there. That's the only way. Now then, shoot, let's get crazy. Don't fight it. Use it. Use it to your advantage. Allow those colors to just come together. Just make a decision and pop them in. In your world you can do anything you want to do. It's just that easy. That easy. Just let things happen, evolve. Don't worry about it. Just get an idea in your mind. Let it go. Drop it in wherever. Everything's not great in life. I tell you what, let's get crazy. In your world you sort of make a big decision and just drop it in."

In the end Ross created a landscape painting with a steel-colored lake and snow-streaked trees illuminated by an iridescent citrus-hued winter sunset. Underneath it all was the painted-over yellow mushroom cloud, diffused into the sky. The episode opened up space for the atomic uncanny to emerge, what Joe Masco refers to as a "perceptual space caught between apocalyptic experience and sensory fulfillment."[56] Under the influence of *The Joy of Painting*, I felt as if I had entered the painted-televisual scene and that I was "suffused, like a cloud, with the riotous colors of the world of pictures."[57] I felt as if Bob Ross had painted this atom bomb in me as just another "happy accident."

NEUTRON-IRRADIATED DIME

"Early on, I learned to disguise myself in words, which really were [mushroom] clouds."[58] The words I used made me similar to the things around me in Oak Ridge. They were rigid yet buoyed by myth. Inside gridded notebooks featuring pale-blue lines I sketched worlds of Smoky Mountain people, atomic spies, and detective stories set in California. I was obsessed with the otherness of the West Coast; I dreamed California—so much so that my Golden State stories were written by L.A. Freeman and set in Los Angeles.[59]

The California stories shared a plot device wherein the protagonist (L.A.) always carried a quarter for an emergency phone call (this is what a pay phone call cost in the 1980s). The quarter was never used for this purpose: it never clinked in the coin slot, never once produced a dial tone. Instead, the chin of George Washington, resting on the word LIBERTY, would blind attackers by focusing the sun's rays, or the coin's rough outer ridges would help it lodge in the throat of an attack dog or eat away at ropes binding hands tied behind chairs.

My mountain stories were lighter copies of my grandmother's dark Appalachian ones. Disfigurement featured prominently in these tales, as did evil. Beauty was often on the inside of the characters and places, but even that was twisted. Lines and plots were distorted in my telling, both from a lack of skill but also from something else. My grandmother's tales were neater; she had a clearer sense of the good and the necessary.

Later I began to write stories about Oak Ridge. I would write about the mountain folks who came down into the valley to work on the bomb, along with Russian spies, atomic detectives, mad scientists, and not-mad scientists. In these stories the plot device shifted from a quarter to an irradiated dime from the museum in Oak Ridge: fifteen cents less on the surface but inside the curled potential of the atom. The power of the neutron-irradiated dime was weak in the pocket, but it was a power that concentrated the atomic past, a power that also was cloaked in the word LIBERTY.

UNDERGROUND GRANDPARENTS

There is an Oak Ridge above the surface and another, its secret twin, below. When I was eleven, I wrote a short story about these twinned towns, a disaster-tinged utopia called "Oak Ridge under Oak Ridge." I learned much later that the French sociologist Gabriel Tarde wrote his own story of doubled worlds—stacked one on top of the other, like bunk beds—nearly a century earlier. Tarde's text of subterranean speculative fiction was called *Underground Man*. It was set in a neo–Ice Age, a post-catastrophic time of cold and darkness after the sun was mysteriously choked. My story, so fitting for the American fears of the eighties, was set in the aftermath of a Soviet nuclear attack. Because of nuclear winter everything on the surface of Oak Ridge seeped downwards in what Tarde might call the "diffusion of innovations": the laboratories, the Cemestos, the Olympic-sized swimming pool, and even my grandmother's hammock were relocated below the earth, only without the Japanese maples that held it in suspension—left above, they'd been vaporized. I imagined my grandparents living below the earth as slightly paler versions of themselves: Underground Frank and Underground Nan bowling, tinkering, and drinking coffee on the inverted ridge.

TWO PHOTOGRAPHS, MARCH AND APRIL 1968

My grandfather kept a small burgundy photo album in his workshop. I liked to leaf through it as I watched him work. Most of the photos were of family members—my brother, my cousins, my grandmother hamming it up for the camera—but two mysterious black-and-white snaps featured the ghost-white eighteen-wheeler that my grandfather drove during his tenure as an atomic courier for the AEC. One photo depicts the truck up close: the machine looks alive and friendly; the headlights are round and seemingly innocent, the driver's-side door is open in a welcoming gesture, and the wheels are turned toward the camera (and the person looking). There is a black-framed rectangle below the windshield containing the word "White" written in script. Another, lower rectangle contains the symbols "US Government, E-01042." The strangest element is a man in a fedora popping up through the top of the cab. His face is hidden by shadow but I know the man is my grandfather, and in this photo he appears as Athena, the goddess of handicraft and warfare, who was born from the head of Zeus.

The second photo shows the same truck from a distance. It was this one that gave a real sense of the vehicle's size and length, something that could not have been grasped from the first photo alone. The experience of taking in these two images together is like looking at a dachshund from the front and then from the side. A semi-trailer truck and a wiener dog both need to be observed from at least two angles to really appreciate them.

In the second photograph, the truck sits parked in a western landscape, mountainous and dotted with small, scrubby plants. Half the photograph is washed in black (a photographer's mistake? a thumb over the viewfinder? a shutter only half open?). The effect heightens the unknowableness of the image: not in terms of what is outside the frame, which we often talk about with photographs,

MAR • 68 •

APR 68 •

but the absolute mystery of what is inside the 3.5-inch by 3.5-inch square. We can't know what the whiteness of the truck contains. Fellow drivers on the interstate in the spring of 1968 couldn't know, either; they were unaware that dangerous things were zooming along the road beside them. Nor did my grandfather know: that information was above his security clearance. What we do know is that these two photographs document trips along the atomic highway stretching from Oak Ridge to Los Alamos or maybe to Hanford and back again.

When I think about these photographs, I think about my grandfather being irradiated as he drove (many couriers were). I think of him in the regular course of his work irradiating the highway, irradiating all of America. I think of him trucking across the land in the government's enormous Wite-Out bottle on wheels attempting to obscure the very phrases it was writing with its tires—driving the conspicuously inconspicuous machine, trying hard to say "Nothing to see here."

A TAMER OF FOXES TAMES NO WOLVES[60]

A brown shoebox in the hall closet revealed a strange series of photographs from the late 1960s of my grandmother posing flamboyantly on her lawn. Time stamps mark them as August 1966, June 1968, and July 1968, but they seem like they were taken the same day, a day full of costume changes, entirely in the character of my grandmother. The exposures are poor and the images are fuzzy, as in a dream. In each she wears a dress and a large hat that accents her tall mountain frame. In each she holds a fox pelt. The implied meaning of the pelt shifts depending on how Nan holds it—from a drape to a pet to a kill.

In the first photograph she is dressed almost all in black, including dark sunglasses. A reddish bow across her midsection provides a flash of color, and off her right arm hangs the orange-red fox pelt, a limp and languid accessory.

In the second photograph she wears a dark-orange dress that she has drawn on with a Sharpie. Just below her collarbones, there is a circle, meant to be a bowling ball. The roughly sketched shape fills the space on her chest where superheroes often have their identifying symbol. Inside Nan has written the word "SPARE." Bowling pins

rendered in black marker arc off each side, flanking her breasts. Below she has drawn another large circle, another bowling ball, over her stomach, and inside she has written in capital letters "IF I PASS OUT NOTIFY MY *CAPTAIN* MARGE O." Paper bowling pins affixed to her hat and nylons bookend the look. Almost unnoticeable against the clamor of the outfit, the fox pelt is held sweetly in the crook of her left arm. This is the only photograph of the series where the fox seems as if it could be alive: its head points to the side; it appears alert.

The last photograph shows the most swagger. Nan's hair is full and glamorous, a no-nonsense look defines her face, and there is nothing jokey about her outfit. In a floral dress, with her hip cocked and her right arm parallel to the ground, she holds out the fox pelt, as if for inspection. The animal's nose points lifelessly to the grass below.

In Barthes's terminology the snapshots are full of *punctum*, the parts of a photograph that prick, wound, and hit us personally, and light on *studium*, the elements of a photograph that deliver cultural, historical, and social context. If the *studium*, as Barthes writes, "is a kind of education,"[61] what is to be learned from the photographs of Nan remains unclear. These images of my grandmother in summer, on a lawn, with the remnants of a dead fox, pierce me over and over like a skilled archer emptying a full quiver of arrows. In their wake, I become a Saint Sebastian of looking.

Then a story arrives, seemingly unrelated. Very soon after I discovered these photos, my uncle told me that when my grandfather worked for the AEC, they used to drive around the atomic reservation shooting foxes. This wasn't for sport but rather a somber task ordered by the government. They would toss the dead foxes in the back of the truck and deliver them to a side door at the lab. My grandfather never knew why, but he speculated that the foxes might be radioactive. He never asked a superior to confirm his theory; he simply followed the order. This scrap of information from my uncle made me wonder if the pelt in the photographs came from the atomic reservation, if a Geiger counter had scanned its still-warm body, and if later, when cool and scraped of its vitality, the pelt had been returned to my grandfather and then gifted to my grandmother.

WOLFHOOD (AFTER CARL SANDBURG)

There is a wolf in me. I keep this wolf because Oak Ridge gave it to me and Oak Ridge will not let it go.[62] I found this wolf in the bushes of my Oak Ridges of hope. It is the same wolf that devoured me when I was young. I gobbled it up in return. Now the wolf is inside me, lounging among my soft pink organs, shifting them as it sees fit. My grandmother is in there too, twisted in a human-lupine snuggle. Wolves and hopes are things that shape-shift.

SUMMER EVENINGS

On long summer evenings Melton Lake held the light, just as it held the grey heron's dainty feet. I jogged along the shore in waffle-soled Nikes, making square patterns on the dirt path. I carried on around the bend, past the red gates of the Chinese restaurant, zipping by the concrete athleticism of the rowing station until I hit the straighter path that would take me to the yellow-lined turnpike and then to my grandparents' house, where I would stop and rest. Still red-faced from running, I would lean against the black-walnut tree, where I delighted in rubbing the feathery leaves between my thumb and forefinger to release their lemon-scented smell. By such increments summer entered my body. Finally exhausted, I sprawled in the grass, arms stretched out, crucified by laziness. Another summer evening in Oak Ridge, Tennessee, "in the time I lived there so successfully disguised to myself a child."[63]

MORRISTOWN: SUMMER 1988

In the blue hour, when earth and sky began to merge, when moths fell from the lampposts like snow, when the peacocks across the street stopped screaming, when the dog settled down with a sleepy howl, when the parents had unwound, slightly: this is when we emerged from our dens to play spy versus spy. We cut across the lawns, creating shortcuts, paths of smashed grass, what architect's call desire lines. We moved slowly so as not to give ourselves away; we were a smattering of delicate predators in search of "Soviets" hiding in our midst.

RECTANGLES (FOR ROBYN O'NEIL)

I was born of rectangles,[64] but I moved to a place I took to be formless or ugly (which I thought of as the same thing). I was born of a gridded order that could not fail, but I moved to a place gone soft, even from its ruralness. I was born from the ghosts of the Manhattan Project, but I ended up in a spectral architecture where dreams of a Skymart led to nowhere. I was born from fissionable isotopes but went to school in a town almost made famous for Little League. I was born from the hard drives of supercomputers but went on field trips to Davy Crockett's daddy's reconstructed tavern. I was born from those who were born from the bomb, but I ended up where *The Evil Dead* was filmed.

CULTURAL ORIGAMI

As I eased into my teenage years, I organized myself into forms that would get me by the paper tigers of my town. I bent myself into an origami of culturally acceptable shapes.

RUBIK'S CUBE

In the 1980s, Ernő Rubik, an architecture professor from Budapest, Hungary, created a mania for puzzle solving with his magic cube. The little cube could be found in almost every ordinary American home with a resident under twenty. At first Rubik's cube inspired people to line up the colors and create a lovely order out of the jumble. I never made it that far. My cube transformed from an odd collection of bright colors to a different odd collection of bright colors. Some, so obsessed with fixing the disorder or with a need to demonstrate their dominion over this small object, took it apart with pocketknives or screwdrivers and rearranged the cubes; others peeled off the stickers and swapped them, sometimes leaving telltale signs of snaily adhesive or rumpled, wrinkly colors.

This is not what Rubik intended. His father was a flight engineer and his mother a poet; he was interested in both how movement works and how it could be represented. He thought of his cube as an artwork, a moving sculpture, and a model for thinking. I learned from Donna Haraway that "a model is a work object; a model is not the same *kind* of thing as a metaphor or an analogy. A model is worked, and it does work. A model is like a miniature cosmos . . . the complex-enough, simple-enough world."[65] Rubik's cube was designed for his students to contemplate objects in space, to think about how these positions change things and how this small square with its deceptively simple design could work as a stand-in for human spatiotemporal relationships. Rubik conceived the idea for his cube while watching water flow around stones in the Danube River. With his teaching shoes on and his

briefcase knocking against his legs, he raced to his mother's house, where he made a wooden prototype, held together by rubber bands.[66]

Rubik wanted his cube to please those who encountered it with its complexity and simple beauty, its potential for stability or chaos, and its challenge. The Rubik's cube has 43,252,003,274,489,856,000 (43 quintillion) possible positions: the "solved" position is merely one of them. Americans did not understand this; we were afflicted with the longing to solve. Others, more dexterous than I, started to work the puzzle faster and faster—speedcubers emerged. Then folks blindfolded themselves before solving the puzzle; they were called blindcubers. National and international competitions were held. But Rubik's battles were not only for the most highly skilled; they trickled down to the lowest levels. Cubing challenges were all the rage in my elementary school. They took place during lunch; sometimes bets were placed, some-times cookies were lost in payment. The cubes turned and turned, propelled by an American lust for order, speed, and mastery. All the while, my hopelessly unsolved cube sat on a little white dresser, next to a small world globe and a snowglobe, making for an accidental museum to dreaming and disorder.

HYPERCOLOR

In the green haze of Appalachian summer, we ran through the yard wearing Hypercolor shirts that revealed some of the warmest spots on our bodies.[67] The t-shirts accentu-ated the truth that colors are not only known visually but are also felt. The outline of a hand made by the touch of a crush's hot palm was a status symbol, a mark of desire and of being desired. The absence of evidence of preteen mitts upon us or the nonexistence of our own handprints touching others made us a kind of invisible, a failure, un-able to make our mark. The wrong hot hands coming into contact with our cottons turned us into a spectacle; our faces showed our heat in a telling blush. On the lawn, in the sun, our desire was let loose; and as it was freed, it was closely monitored. In the warm afternoons, these cruel shirts—one color when cool, another when hot—chromatically announced that some of us ran hotter than others. I was one of the cooler ones then; the hue of my shirt was often resistant to change, and I was less likely to warm the shirts of others, which held its own kind of shame.

RADIOACTIVE FROGGER

In 1991, about one hundred radioactive frogs escaped from a pond containing legacy nuclear waste from ORNL. When the incident was reported in the news, the measurement of the radioactivity sounded mysterious—a thousand disintegrations per minute—like something coming apart quickly.

It actually took a while for the conditions of the escape to materialize. For decades, on the grounds of ORNL, Canadian geese congregated on the edge of the pond, as great blue herons nested nearby. The geese nibbled on a variety of insects and grasses, while the herons ate the small frogs that made their homes in the radioactive mud. In the late 1980s, scientists discovered that some of the goose shit scattered around the city was hot. In response, they covered the pond with wire mesh to keep the birds away. It didn't matter so much about the geese, but without the herons the frog population grew exponentially.

Eventually there wasn't enough space in the pond and the frogs started to wriggle out. Some workers at ORNL accidently ran over the creatures with their cars and trucks, causing their tires to become radioactive. People started talking about the creatures' efforts to escape as a game of radioactive Frogger. And then all I could see was the Atari game I played with my brother, sitting cross-legged on the floor of his bedroom. I thought about how bad I was at video games and how I could never prevent my frogs from ending up as roadkill, smashed by the brightly colored vehicles. Game Over.

Fueled by nuclear fantasies and the lure of radioactive amphibians, the national news media descended on Oak

Ridge, expecting three-eyed creatures with hideous deformities. Many were disappointed with what they saw: tiny leopard frogs with long skinny legs just where they should be, no different in appearance from other common frogs. The nuclear imagination had animated the reporters, and the Associated Press spread it across America. A folksinger wrote a song about it with a jokey tone that felt off to me.

Years later the folksinger became a Unitarian Universalist minister and wrote a very sincere song about Hiroshima.[68] The crushed frogs from ORNL were disposed of as radioactive waste. I don't know what became of the herons.

THE FAR SIDE

When I was young, I began each new day by ripping off a sheet on my daily *The Far Side* calendar. I delighted in visiting the gonzo world created by the cartoonist Gary Larson, featuring women in horned-rimmed glasses, rotund middle-aged men, nerdy children, and a menagerie of thoughtful animals. Many of these cartoons stand out clearly in my memory. There's the one where the kid is pushing on the door that says "PULL" in front of the Midvale School for the Gifted. Another depicts a happy guy in hell whistling, as one devil says to another, "You know, we're just not reaching that guy." My favorite shows enemy forces welcomed into a castle disguised as a huge wiener dog: *The Far Side*'s take on the Trojan horse. Gary Larson's cartoons were clever, offbeat, and occasionally macabre.

One of Larson's darkest drawings depicts a post-human world after a nuclear attack. In the foreground five happy bugs dance in a circle on a leaf. The arrangement of the dancing insects resembles that of the dancers in Matisse's famous painting *The Dance*. Behind the twirling insects there is a series of rolling hills, then a city being torn apart. Buildings crumble, signifying the end of that city—maybe of all cities. The bugs seem intoxicated by the disorienting power of the three mushroom clouds exploding in the distance. The human world hangs in apocalyptic abeyance as the joyous insects dream of the world to come.

Although Larson's scene was rendered in simple black and white, what frightened me as a child was that I could easily imagine a colorful nuclear explosion. As a grandchild of the bomb, I was trained by culture to see the brilliant colors of atomic explosions, even when they were not there. I could envision the colorful series that made up a nuclear blast, moving from deep reds to yellowy oranges, only to be obscured by whites, then followed by dark grays and blacks in the final stages of the spectacular mushroom cloud and the beginnings of fallout. I could see in my mind's eye an "overpowering climax of luminosity," as Matisse once described his painting of brightly colored dancers.[69]

ATOMIC FIREBALLS

As a kid, I went through a phase when sometimes after school I smoked clandestinely behind the 7-Eleven. Stallion was my brand of choice. The packaging had two black beauties galloping across an open white expanse under a solid stripe of red. The logo was a bit crude, and one of the horse's legs was bent at an impossible angle. Still, the running equine image combined with the illicit activity made

me feel free. With a stallion in my hand, I had the perfect prop to act the detective, the rebel, the spy.

My mother didn't allow candy cigarettes; later they were banned by the state. Those in favor of the ban argued that candy cigarettes romanticized smoking and that playing at smoking could provide a gateway to the real and dangerous practice. When I could no longer pretend at smoking, I took up Atomic Fireballs as my candy of choice. Atomic Fireballs were bright-red cinnamon-flavored jaw-breakers with a corpse-white core. "Red. Hot. Flavor. The original super intense cinnamon candy! 15 million of these spicy gems are consumed every week around the world. Kids dare each other to eat them . . . one after another after another. How much hot can you handle?" This was the dare of sweet proliferation that the Ferrara Pan company peddled.

The experience of eating these candies was often one of too-muchness, a tingling, burning sensation on the tongue. Those little spheres would get too hot, and I would have to take them out of my mouth for a break, holding them between my thumb and forefinger. Atomic Fireballs were never banned, never even controversial. My mom thought they were fine but that it was tacky to take half-eaten candy out of your mouth and put it back in. The cinnamon candies, which I imagined to be radioactive, were part of my atomic socialization, part of how I came to understand that the atomic was a wild challenge to win. Through my little candies, I learned that with practice and perseverance, the atomic could be controlled. The benefits outweighed the costs. How much hot could I handle?[70]

ADAM BOMB

I was a miniature collector, a smaller version of Edward Fuchs. I had an electric-blue Trapper Keeper filled with Garbage Pail Kids.[71] The grotesque cards depicted children with rhyming or approximately rhyming names: Boney Tony, unzipping his face to reveal a cracked skull underneath; Snowy Joey, being suffocated inside a menacing snow globe; Deaf Geoff, a cool kid in an inky-black motorcycle jacket with a boom box to his ear, the power of the music exploding half of his face, his eyes, mouth, and pink brain flying out with musical notes; and dozens of others like these. Set side by side the cards could function as the school photographs of an elementary school in hell.

The Garbage Pail Kids illustrated all kinds of terrible things that could happen to a person, hundreds of our unconscious fears laid out in bright colors.[72] They smelled sweetly stale because of the brittle piece of pink bubble gum that came, like a stowaway, in their packaging. They were malleable macabre objects—they could be kept as a card or peeled off as a sticker and stuck almost anywhere. Like kudzu, they covered the landscape of my youth. Some teachers and parents felt the situation had gotten out of hand: Garbage Pail Kids were banned from school. After the ban I had to work in secret sneaking them out during recess.

When my mother picked me up from school, with my brother already sitting in the front seat, I could slide into the back and work out in the open. There I would reorganize my collection, making sure not to bend the cardboard edges as they slid into their plastic envelopes (I never used them as stickers). I kept my Garbage Pail Kids organized in

alphabetical order. The first card, my favorite and the one that scared me most, was Adam Bomb. He was a little kid, but he wore a dark-blue suit with a yellow-and-red striped tie; he looked like the guy from AC/DC. He had his finger on a red button, pressing it, the top of his head exploding into a mushroom cloud, his blue eyes glassy, a lazy smile on his face.

My blue eyes would fall on his to find that he was always already pressing the button: the pressing created an explosion but also a pause. It exploded the continuum of history.[73] The pressing was a warning of what could happen and a reminder of what already had. Riding in the back seat of the twentieth century, I was acutely aware of the destructive power of nuclear technologies.

ATOMIC COURIERS

I was born under the atom-acorn totem of Oak Ridge. As an adult, I move through the world with its image inked on my left forearm. Following my grandfather, I am also a kind of atomic courier; I carry and disseminate the secret messages of atomic Appalachia through living, speaking, and writing about where I am from.

ROLAND BARTHES, LITTLE RED RIDING HOOD, AND THE WOLF

I keep returning to Barthes and his claim that we cannot contest our own culture without understanding the limits of our language and situated knowledge, that to do so is like trying to rid ourselves of the wolf from a comfortable perch inside the animal.[74] But who says we want out, or away, or to be rid of this wolf? As Djuna Barnes insists: "Children know something they can't tell; they like Red Riding Hood and the wolf in bed!"[75]

This struggling with the idea of the atomic and its hold on me is something I like, something terrifying but not without its pleasures. There is pleasure in the writing and in the thinking from alongside or even inside the wolf. There I can be with my grandmother, both of us duped by the gray-bearded beast, devoured whole, and hanging out together in his red velvet insides.

THIS ATOM BOMB IN ME

When Walter Benjamin was writing about his Berlin childhood, he developed a theory that suggested that the things we are surrounded by when we are young are formed inside us, absorbed. As we "wander through the world of things," he writes, they first seem mysterious, "like the stations of a journey of whose extent we can form no conception." Slowly, over time, as we confront these familiar objects, we take them in, feel our places within and among them, even feel part of them. Benjamin connects these things inside us, accrued during our childhood, to our abilities to perform mimetically, a power that is enhanced by memory and "southern moonlit nights," which can create a kind of "force field."[76]

Benjamin meant something different by "southern" than I do—his southern landscape was likely Ibiza or Naples, places far away from atomic Appalachia—but his suggestion of a connection between childhood memories and a kind of force field resonates. This force field, which for Benjamin is nearly cosmic, emerges from a power to be like those things that surround us. It is a feeling of connectedness that emerges when we find ourselves in places shot through with memory. In these places we feel a part of things, and we feel things from those places as a part of us, too.

Growing up in the atomic sensorium, I felt something akin to Benjamin's force field. I felt animated by a kind of power coming from Oak Ridge and my connection to the Atomic City. I often felt like the acorn inside the twirling atom, the city's totem—something ordinary made extraordinary through a field of power. Sometimes my feelings of connection with the objects and spaces of my childhood were more complicated: they interrupted this smooth spinning. In these moments of interruption, or as Fred Moten might say, hesitation, I felt a sense of vulnerability combined with an attraction I struggled to understand. I think of Barthes and realize that along with the moments of pleasure and the warm feeling of power, there were always moments when I was uncomfortable inside the wolf. There were times when I was uneasy inside an unhesitating, overly confident culture built on the principles of Atoms for Peace and Mutual Assured Destruction. Today, these uncomfortable feelings are only more pronounced. I have become keenly attuned to the creepy and creeping resonances of an atmosphere of danger that is sometimes merely a weak sensation and sometimes completely overwhelming in nuclear things and places. I have become hyperaware of the atom bomb inside me. On anxious days, I feel it ticking, keeping pace with the hands on the Doomsday Clock reaching for midnight.[77]

ACKNOWLEDGMENTS

Early seeds of this book appeared as "Atomic Childhood around 1980," in "Memory | Materiality | Sensuality," special issue, *Memory Studies 9,* no. 1 (2016): 75–84.

Special thanks to Emily-Jane Cohen, who believed in this project from the beginning. Plus huge thanks to Faith Wilson Stein and the rest of the folks at Stanford University Press.

For their thinking, writing, and support, I would like to thank my parents, Gloria Haynes Brown and the whole Haynes family, Leslie Bernstein and Lauren Packard, the Black Mountain School, Jon Horne Carter, and Dara Culhane and the Centre for Imaginative Ethnography; plus all my lovely colleagues on the sci-fi mountain of Simon Fraser University, especially Ann Travers; Karen Engle, writing from the tunnels below Moose Jaw; Barbara Ferrell, an Oak Ridge institution; Graeme Gilloch; Susan Lepselter, whose writing keeps resonating in my brain; William Mazzerella, for helping me think through the atom-acorn totem; Fred Moten, for critical poetry; The Octopus, Ben Nienass and Rachel Daniell, always; Robyn O'Neil; Coleman Nye, for reading and coming to understand the wolf; Allen Shelton, for the Monk's Manhattans and the pretty writing; Katie Stewart, for making different kinds of writing seem possible; Mick Taussig and The Convolutes, kindred spirits; Stéphane Valognes, Jean-Marc Fournier, and the Uni-Caen stay-weird crew; Yoke-Sum Wong and the Alberta School; and Zazie, my editing companion and the creature who heard more about this project than anyone.

And most of all, I would like to thank Jessi Lee Jackson, who makes a writing and reading life more possible, lovely, and fun than I could have imagined.

NOTES

1. For more on the nuclear heritage tourism industry, see Freeman, *Longing for the Bomb: Oak Ridge and Atomic Nostalgia*; Hodge and Weinberger, *A Nuclear Family Vacation: Travels in the World of Atomic Weaponry*; Vanderbilt, *Survival City: Adventures among the Ruins of Atomic America*; and Wray, "A Blast from the Past: Preserving and Interpreting the Atomic Age."

2. See Bennett, *Vibrant Matter: A Political Ecology of Things.*

3. Williams, "Structures of Feeling"; Hans Speier, "Magic Geography"; Freeman, *Longing for the Bomb.*

4. Barthes, *Empire of Signs*, 8.

5. When thinking with affect here, I follow Sara Ahmed's delightfully gooey, messy framing: "what sticks, or what sustains or preserves the connection between ideas, values, and object." Again, Ahmed: "I do not assume there is something called affect that stands apart or has autonomy . . . Instead I would begin with the messiness of the experiential, the unfolding of bodies into worlds, and the drama of contingency, how we are touched by what we are near." Ahmed, *The Promise of Happiness*, 29–30.

6. For more about mnemonic assemblages, see Freeman; Nienass; and Daniell, "Memory | Materiality | Sensuality," 3.

7. Du Bois, "Sociology Hesitant," 39.

8. Mills, "Sociological Poetry," 125.

9. The quotation can be found in Mills, *Letters and Autobiographical Writings*, 41. Mills' *White Collar* also contains two explicit references to his quest to capture the "tang and the feel":

Yet it is to this white-collar world that one must look for much that is characteristic of twentieth-century existence. By their rise to numerical importance, the white-collar people have upset the nineteenth-century expectation that society would be divided between entrepreneurs and wage workers. By their mass way of life, they have transformed the tang and feel of the American experience. They carry, in a most revealing way, many of those psychological themes that characterize our epoch, and, in one way or another, every general theory of the main drift has had to take account of them. For above all else they are a new cast of actors, performing the major routines of twentieth-century society." (ix)

The salesman's world has now become everybody's world, and, in some part, everybody has become a salesman. The enlarged market has become at once more impersonal and more intimate. What is there that does not pass through the market? Science and love, virtue and conscience, friendliness, carefully nurtured skills and animosities? This is a time of venality. The market now reaches into every institution and every relation. The bargaining manner, the huckstering animus, the memorized theology of pep, the commercialized evaluation of personal traits—they are all around us; in public and in private there is the tang and feel of salesmanship. (161)

Mills felt that this book should be read as a collection of "prose poems."

10. Moten, "Manic Depression: A Poetics of Hesitant Sociology"; email correspondence with Moten, April 16, 2017.

11. I am motivated here by Mills' challenge from *The Sociological Imagination*: "Every [person their] own methodologist! Methodologists! Get to work!" I am also inspired by Andrew Abbott's discussion of lyrical poetry and sociological writing. See Mills, *The Sociological Imagination*, 123; and Abbott, "Against Narrative: A Preface to Lyrical Sociology," 67–99.

12. Following Adorno, I want to insist that "the substance of a poem is not merely an expression of individual impulses and experiences" but rather part and parcel of the social as well. And while I hope to learn something about an atomic Appalachian habitus, I also want to write a text that "enchants the poet-thinkers." Bourdieu might not approve of my methods. See Adorno, "On Lyric Poetry and Society," 38; and Bourdieu, *Sketch for Self-Analysis*, 27.

13. Taussig, *The Nervous System*, 2; Haraway, *Staying with the Trouble: Making Kin in the Chthulucene*, 12

14. McCarthy, *The Road*, 131.

15. The verb "mondrianate" is borrowed from Cortázar, *Hopscotch*, 36.

16. For more on my mother's yellow pantsuit, see Freeman, *Longing for the Bomb*, 92.

17. Beckett, *Proust*, 3–4.

18. See Rogers, "Conflict."

19. Mister Rogers had this quotation from Antoine de Saint-Exupéry's *Le Petit Prince* in its original French—"L'essentiel est invisible pour les yeux"—hanging in a frame in his office for his entire television career.

20. See Rogers, "Death" and "Divorce."

21. See Rogers, "Conflict."

22. Benjamin, "On the Concept of History," 392.

23. Mills, *The Sociological Imagination*, 5.

24. Yellowcake, also called urania, is a type of uranium concentrate powder that has very low radioactivity. This is uranium in an intermediate stage in processing. Yellowcake is valuable because it can be converted into U-235, a more fissionable type of uranium, to be used in nuclear weapons or as fuel for nuclear reactors.

25. Benjamin, *Berlin Childhood around 1900*, 109.

26. Quoted in Bachelard, *The Poetics of Space*, 75.

27. Bachelard points out Bergson's "derogatory" use of the word "drawer" in *The Poetics of Space*, 74; see also Bergson, *Matter and Memory*.

28. Reagan's speech was written by Peggy Noonan. It included lines from the poem "High Flight" by the aviator poet John Gillespie Magee, Jr.

29. Here I'm referring to the original American version of *Captain Atom* from the 1960s, published by Charlton Comics. *Captain Atom* was created by writer Joe Gill and artist and co-writer Steve Ditko, first appearing in *Space Adventures* 1, no. 33 (March 1960), where this quotation appears. The character of Captain Atom was the inspiration for Alan Moore's Dr. Manhattan in *Watchmen* (DC Comics, 1986–1987). There was also an Australian Captain Atom comic, which appeared in January 1948 from Atlas Publications. The Australian Captain Atom wore a full suit of red and a yellow helmet, and he was much beefier than the American Captain Atom. His superpowers included incredibly sensitive atomic-radar hearing, the ability to generate massive amounts of heat, and the ability to shoot firebolts of atomic energy from his hands. His origin story involved his becoming fused with his twin brother, Dr. Bikini Radar, a nuclear physicist, when they were caught in a nuclear blast. The brothers operated from a single body, the dominant presenting personality alternating between them. The Captain Atom comic series was created during a period when Australia had banned imports from the United States in order to aid its postwar recovery. *Atom* was so popular that even after the ban was lifted in the 1950s, it continued to outsell *Superman* in Australia. Sixty-four issues of the Australian *Captain Atom* were published between 1948 and 1954.

30. Wolfe, *Look Homeward, Angel*, 157.

31. Benjamin, "On the Concept of History," 392.

32. Marx and Engels, "Manifesto of the Communist Party," 353.

33. ". . . imagine Sisyphus happy." Camus, *The Myth of Sisyphus*, 123.

34. Quoted in Gordon, *Ghostly Matters: Haunting and the Sociological Imagination*, 17.

35. In total there were five communities that were evacuated to create the city of Oak Ridge during the Manhattan Project: Elza, New Hope, Robertsville, Scarboro, and Wheat. For more on the Ghost of Wheat, see Freeman, *Longing for the Bomb*, 34–35.

36. This phrase is borrowed from Agnes Martin. Martin said that when she first thought of painting the grids she became famous for, she was thinking of "the innocence of trees." See https://www.moma.org/collection/works/78361.

37. Taussig, *The Nervous System*.

38. M. Gladys Evans, interview by Cindy Kelly, Atomic Heritage Foundation, September 21, 2005, Oak Ridge, Tennessee, http://www.manhattanprojectvoices.org/oral-histories/gladys-evans-interview.

39. For more about Laika and other four-legged cosmonauts, see Turkina, *Soviet Space Dogs*.

40. Foucault, "Of Other Spaces."

41. The archaeological record shows the existence of bikini-style garments dating back to before the time of the ancient Romans, but the modern "bikini" appeared on the scene shortly after the end of World War II. Its name emerged out of a competition between two French designers, Jacques Heim and Louis Réard. In the summer of 1946, as Western Europeans began to head to the beaches again after years of war, Heim, a native of the celebrated beach resort Cannes, introduced a tiny, two-piece-style bathing suit called "L'Atome." While European women had been wearing two-piece swimsuits since the 1930s, Heim's design pushed the envelope by its sheer skimpiness. Proud of his creation, Heim hired skywriters to fly over local beaches in order to promote "the world's smallest bathing suit." Just three weeks later, Heim learned that he had competition from Réard, formerly a French automobile engineer who had turned his hand to women's swimsuit design. Réard's design, which he called the "bikini," was very similar to "L'Atome," only slightly smaller and engineered to expose the navel. He also marketed along the French Riviera, both on the beach and in the skies. In direct competition with Heim, his skywriters wrote in praise of the bikini: "Smaller than the smallest bathing suit in the world." According to Réard, "Unless it could be pulled through a wedding ring," it wasn't a real bikini. In the summer of 1946, size mattered, and the name "bikini" stuck.

Both Heim's "L'Atome," and Réard's "bikini" shared an association with the new Atomic Age. Réard called his "four triangles of nothing" a "bikini" after the Bikini Atoll in the Marshall Islands where the U.S. military was testing megaton atomic bombs. The widely publicized tests were known as Operation Crossroads. They were much more powerful than the U.S. military had intended; as a result, several islands became completely uninhabitable owing to radiation, and radioactive sea spray contaminated large swaths of the ocean. Additionally, the test animals confined on ships in the blast area to determine the effects of radioactivity died or suffered terribly; and many U.S. army personnel were also affected by the radiation, their lives shortened by their proximity to the blasts. Réard chose the name "bikini" because he wanted his design to shock the public just as the atomic tests had done. See Lencek and Bosker, *Making Waves: Swimsuits and the Undressing of America*; Le Zotte, "How the Summer of Atomic Bomb Testing Turned the Bikini into a Phenomenon"; and "This Day in History: July 5."

42. Gordon, *Ghostly Matters*, 64.

43. In 1947, Luther Agee, an architectural draftsman for the AEC, designed Installation Dog (Katy's Kitchen) to look like an abandoned barn. It was used to store weapons-grade uranium from May 1948 to May 1949 but was kept guarded until 1955 in case it was needed again. The project was top secret. Like many folks working in Oak Ridge at the time, Agee was required to undergo periodic polygraph testing to ensure he was not revealing sensitive information. Katy's Kitchen stands to this day and is used by environmental scientists involved in testing the DOE's compliance (or noncompliance) with environmental standards.

44. This vignette was inspired by a line from an essay by Katie Stewart in which she writes: "Place is something that throws itself together in moments, things, in aesthetic sensibilities and affective charges." Stewart, "Precarity's Forms," 579.

45. The Nuclear Energy for the Propulsion of Aircraft (NEPA) project operated in Oak Ridge under the AEC during the 1950s. It was ultimately discontinued after being deemed impractical.

46. Historically, about 2 percent of the deer killed in the hunts are too radioactive to leave the ORNL reservation. In the mid-eighties there was a release of strontium-90 in Oak Ridge that resulted in a spike in the number of "hot" deer. Strontium-90 and cesium-137 do not exist in nature; they are anthropogenic radioactive isotopes—hazardous by-products of nuclear fission—that entered the atmosphere on July 16, 1945, with the first nuclear bomb tested in Alamogordo, New Mexico.

47. Was the gray wolf Sabina Spielrein? In *Ghostly Matters*, Avery Gordon writes about the psychoanalyst Sabina Spielrein, whose story fascinates and distracts her from preparing for a conference presentation. Spielrein is most famous for her place in a romantic-intellectual-uncanny triangle that connected her to both Sigmund Freud and Carl Jung. She was Jung's analysand, lover, and protégé, and later a colleague and correspondent of Freud's. During Spielrein's life, her intellect and contributions were not given their due: she theorized the death drive, for example, a good decade before Freud without much notice. Spielrein thought about the uncanny too—and she took it someplace far stranger than did Freud.

In his famous essay "The Uncanny," Freud is frightened by his own image (taken at first to be someone else) when it surprises him in a mirror on a jerky train. When Spielrein sees herself in a mirror, however, she sees herself as a wolf and then questions her wolf-self assemblage directly. After reading Gordon, I was also distracted and haunted by Spielrein. This passage stopped me cold:

I sat down to the work I had earlier planned on doing, that is, reading his [Jung's] paper. After only a few lines I was completely entranced by him again; it struck me as so silly to have to talk with this brilliant person about such trivialities as his own bad manners, when we had so many really interesting topics of discussion . . . In the evening I learned I had done my friend an injustice; that very day he had had a little girl and could not leave his wife. This information was understandably both gratifying and painful, yet I had myself well in hand and went back to work. When I looked at myself in the mirror before going to bed, I was taken aback; that couldn't be me, that stony gray face with the uncannily grim, burning black eyes staring out at me: it was a powerful, baleful wolf that lurked there coldly in the depths and would halt at nothing. "What is it that you want?" I asked myself in horror. Then I saw all the lines in the room go crooked; everything became alien and terrifying. "The great chill is coming . . ."

After this frightening encounter, Spielrein woke up the next morning feeling "transformed." Reflecting on her experience, she jotted down: "The air was cool, and I breathed in the coolness ecstatically." Like Gordon, I found Spielrein's uncanny contagious; she was on my mind when I went to sleep. See Gordon, *Ghostly Matters*, 49–50; and Carotenuto, *A Secret Symmetry: Sabina Spielrein between Jung and Freud*, 19.

48. Proust, *Finding Time Again*, 348.

49. The Waffle House has its own record label that records music you won't hear on the radio. The lyrics quoted are from Welch, "Waffle House Christmas."

50. Proust, *The Prisoner*, 19.

51. Polenberg, *In the Matter of J. Robert Oppenheimer: The Security Clearance Hearing*, 46.

52. Ross, *The Joy of Painting*.

53. Batchelor, *Chromophobia*, 51.

54. Ross, *The Joy of Painting*.

55. Benjamin, "A Glimpse into the World of Children's Books," 442.

56. Masco, *Nuclear Borderlands: The Manhattan Project in Post–Cold War New Mexico*, 27.

57. Benjamin, "A Glimpse into the World of Children's Books," 435.

58. Walter Benjamin and I really have a thing for cloud imagery. Benjamin, *Berlin Childhood around 1900*, 97.

59. California occupied my mind because I never occupied California, although I almost did. In the early seventies, my parents lived outside San Francisco, briefly. My father was a young psychologist; he had an internship at the same hospital where Ken Kesey wrote *One Flew over the Cuckoo's Nest*. My mother worked at a hospital in Palo Alto, where she watched the second open-heart surgery performed in the United States. They liked California and wished to stay, but Governor Ronald Reagan slashed funding for programs geared toward mental health, so they moved back to Tennessee, where my father had a better chance for work. A few years later my brother and I were born in atomic Appalachia. Reagan was already shaping my life—how and where I would live it—even before I was born.

60. The title of this vignette is an inversion of a line in Carl Phillips' poem "Dirt Being Dirt": "A tamer of wolves tames no foxes."

61. Barthes, *Camera Lucida*, 26.

62. Much here is borrowed from Carl Sandburg's poem "Wilderness."

63. Agee, "Knoxville: Summer 1915," 12.

64. This line from the artist and writer Robyn O'Neil's "Prologue: The War against Fossils" spurred my thinking: "We are not born from rectangles. We just end up in them. Only if we're lucky."

65. Haraway, *Staying with the Trouble*, 63.

66. Rubik, interview by Dave Simpson.

67. The Generra Sportswear Company manufactured Hypercolor clothing, with its special "metamorphic color system." Hypercolor clothes were dyed twice, once with permanent dye and then with thermochromic pigments, which enabled the garments to be one color when warm and another when cool.

68. Small, "Hot Frogs on the Loose" and "Cranes over Hiroshima."

69. Quotation taken from a postcard of Matisse's *Dance (1)*, Museum of Modern Art, New York City, 1980.

70. Nello Ferrara created Atomic Fireballs in 1954 when the United States and the Soviet Union were trying to outdesign each other with more and more powerful thermonuclear weapons. In that same year, at Bikini Atoll in the Marshall Islands, the United States detonated the largest nuke it ever tested, as part of its Castle Bravo series of nuclear tests. Because the weather changed unexpectedly at the time of Bravo's detonation, and because the explosion turned out to be two and a half times greater than planned, fallout from the test was much wider spread than had been an-

ticipated. Nuclear fallout from the fifteen-megaton bomb blanketed the inhabited islands that had not been evacuated. A Japanese fishing boat, the *Fifth Lucky Dragon*, was also contaminated by fallout. Fish from local waters became so radioactive that when placed on photographic plates they could take their own pictures; for an example, see https://commons.wiki media.org/wiki/File:Crossroads_Radioactive_Puffy_Surgeon_Fish.jpg.

71. Eduard Fuchs was a German writer, collector, and historian (1870–1940). My thinking on the grotesque here is influenced by Benjamin's analysis of Fuchs' work *Tang-Plastik* in his essay "Eduard Fuchs, Collector and Historian." Benjamin pulls a quote from Fuchs that can be applied to the Garbage Pail Kids:

> The grotesque is the intense heightening of what is sensually imaginable. In this sense, grotesque figures are an expression of the robust health of an age . . . Yet one cannot dispute the fact that the motivating forces of the grotesque have a crass counterpoint. Decadent times and sick brains also incline toward grotesque representations. In such cases the grotesque is a shocking reflection of the fact that for the times and individuals in question, the problems of the world and of existence appear insoluble. One can see at a glance which of these two tendencies is the creative force behind a grotesque fantasy. (271)

Accordingly, the Garbage Pail Kids are either an expression of health or evidence that the problems of the world and living are unsolvable.

72. During the time Art Spiegelman was turning out Garbage Pail Kids, he was also at work on his Pulitzer Prize–winning graphic novel *Maus I: A Survivor's Tale*. We can imagine some of the darkest moments of the twentieth century spread out on his drawing table alongside afflicted, tortured, and mutilated children made cartoonish.

73. Benjamin, "On the Concept of History," 395.

74. Barthes, *Empire of Signs*, 8.

75. Barnes, *Nightwood*, 79.

76. Benjamin, "The Lamp," 692.

77. The Doomsday Clock first appeared on the cover of the Bulletin of Atomic Scientists in 1947 in order to communicate to political leaders and the public at large the danger and urgency that nuclear weapons posed. The hands of the clock move both clockwise and counterclockwise, depending on atomic scientists' assessment of the chances of nuclear disaster. As I finish this book, the hands on the Doomsday Clock have moved to two and a half minutes from midnight, the closest they have been since the early 1980s.

REFERENCES

Songs

Father John Misty. "Holy Shit." Recorded in Los Angeles, 2013–2014. Track 10 on *I Love You, Honeybear*. Sub Pop.

Mandrell, Barbara, and George Jones. "I Was Country When Country Wasn't Cool." Recorded in Nashville, March 1981. Track 11 on *Barbara Mandrell Live*. MCA Nashville.

Parton, Dolly. "9 to 5." Recorded in Nashville, 1980. Track 5 on *9 to 5 and Odd Jobs*. RCA.

────. "PMS Blues." Recorded at DollyWood, 1994. Track 23 on *Heartsongs: Live from Home*. Columbia Records.

Perkins, Carl. "Tennessee." Recorded in Nashville, 1956. Track 5 on *Original Golden Hits*. Sun Records.

REM. "It's the End of the World as We Know It (And I Feel Fine)." Recorded in Nashville, 1987. Track 6 on *Document*. I.R.S.

Small, Fred. "Cranes over Hiroshima." Recorded in Cambridge, MA, 1985. Track 5 on *No Limit*. Rounder Records.

────. "Hot Frogs on the Loose." Recorded in Cambridge, 1993. Tracks 5 and 6 on *Everything Possible: Fred Small in Concert*. Flying Fish.

Welch, Mary. "Waffle House Christmas." Recorded in Atlanta, 2000. Waffle Records.

Films

Kagan, Jeremy, dir. *The Journey of Natty Gann*. 1985; Burbank: Walt Disney Pictures.

Raimi, Sam, dir. *Evil Dead*. 1981; Beverly Hills: Renaissance Pictures.

Television

Rogers, Fred. "Conflict." *Mister Rogers' Neighborhood*, episodes 1521–1525, aired November 7–11, 1983. National Educational Television and Radio Center.

────. "Death." *Mister Rogers' Neighborhood*, episode 1101, aired March 23, 1970. National Educational Television and Radio Center.

────. "Divorce." *Mister Rogers' Neighborhood*, episode 1477, aired February 17, 1981. National Educational Television and Radio Center.

Ross, Bob. *The Joy of Painting*, season 17, episode 6, February 9, 1989, PBS.

Texts

Abbott, Andrew. "Against Narrative: A Preface to Lyrical Sociology." *Sociological Theory* 25, no. 1 (2007): 67–99.

Adorno, Theodor. "On Lyric Poetry and Society." In *Notes to Literature*, vol. 1, translated by Shierry Weber Nicholsen, 37–54. New York: Columbia University Press, 1991.

Agee, James. "Knoxville: Summer 1915." Prologue to *A Death in the Family*. St. Albans, UK: Panther Books, 1973.

Agee, James, and Walker Evans. *Let Us Now Praise Famous Men*. New York: Mariner Books, 2001.

Ahmed, Sara. *The Promise of Happiness*. Durham, NC: Duke University Press, 2010.

Augé, Marc. *Oblivion*. Minneapolis: University of Minnesota Press, 2004.

Bachelard, Gaston. *The Poetics of Reverie*. Boston: Beacon Press, 1969.

────. *The Poetics of Space*. Boston: Beacon Press, 1994.

Barnes, Djuna. *Nightwood*. New York: New Directions, 2006.

Barthes, Roland. *Camera Lucida*. New York: Hill & Wang, 1980.

────. *Empire of Signs*. New York: Hill & Wang, 1982.

Batchelor, David. *Chromophobia*. London: Reaktion Books, 2001.

Beckett, Samuel. *Proust*. New York: Grove Press, 1978.

Benjamin, Walter. *Berlin Childhood around 1900*. Cambridge, MA: Belknap Press of Harvard University Press, 2006.

────. "Eduard Fuchs, Collector and Historian." In *Selected Writings*, vol. 3, *1935–1938*, 260–302. Cambridge, MA: Belknap Press of Harvard University Press, 2002.

────. "A Glimpse into the World of Children's Books." In *Selected*

Writings, vol. 1, *1913–1926*, 435–443. Cambridge, MA: Belknap Press of Harvard University Press, 2004.

———. "The Lamp." In *Selected Writings*, vol. 2, *1913–1926*, 691–693. Cambridge, MA: Belknap Press of Harvard University Press, 2005.

———. "On the Concept of History." In *Selected Writings*, vol. 4, *1938–1940*, 389–400. Cambridge, MA: Belknap Press of Harvard University Press, 2003.

———. *On Hashish*. Edited by Howard Eiland. Cambridge, MA: Belknap Press of Harvard University Press, 2006.

Benjamin, Walter [pseud.]. *Recent Writings*. Vancouver, BC: New Documents, 2013.

Bennett, Jane. *Vibrant Matter: A Political Ecology of Things*. Durham, NC: Duke University Press, 2010.

Bergson, Henri. *Matter and Memory*. Cambridge, MA: MIT Press, 1991.

Bourdieu, Pierre. *Sketch for Self-Analysis*. Chicago: University of Chicago Press, 2008.

Camus, Albert. *The Myth of Sisyphus*. New York: Vintage, 1991.

Carotenuto, Aldo. *A Secret Symmetry: Sabina Spielrein between Jung and Freud*. New York: Pantheon Books, 1984.

Carson, Anne. *Nox*. New York: New Directions, 2010.

Cortázar, Julio. *Hopscotch*. New York: Random House, 1966.

Du Bois, W. E. B. "Sociology Hesitant." *boundary 2* 27, no. 3 (2000): 37–44.

Evans, M. Gladys. Interview by Cindy Kelly. Atomic Heritage Foundation, September 21, 2005. Oak Ridge, Tennessee. http://www.manhattanprojectvoices.org/oral-histories/gladys-cvans interview.

Foucault, Michel. "Of Other Spaces." *Diacritics* 16 (Spring 1986): 22–27.

Freeman, Lindsey. "Atomic Childhood around 1980." *Memory Studies* 9, no. 1 (2016): 75–84.

———. *Longing for the Bomb: Oak Ridge and Atomic Nostalgia*. Chapel Hill: University of North Carolina Press, 2015.

Freeman, Lindsey, Benjamin Nienass, and Rachel Daniell. "Memory | Materiality | Sensuality." *Memory Studies* 9, no. 1 (2016): 3–12.

Freud, Sigmund. "The Uncanny." In *The Standard Edition of the Complete Psychological Works of Sigmund Freud*, vol. 17: *An Infantile Neurosis and Other Works (1917–1919)*, 217–256. London: The Hogarth Press and The Institute of Psycho-Analysis, 1955.

Gill, Joe, writer, and Steve Ditko, artist. *Space Adventures #33*. Derby, CT: Charlton Comics, 1960.

Gordon, Avery. *Ghostly Matters: Haunting and the Sociological Imagination*. Minneapolis: University of Minnesota Press, 2008.

Haraway, Donna. *Staying with the Trouble: Making Kin in the Chthulucene*. Durham, NC: Duke University Press, 2016.

Hodge, Nathan, and Sharon Weinberger. *A Nuclear Family Vacation: Travels in the World of Atomic Weaponry*. New York: Bloomsbury, 2008.

Kesey, Ken. *One Flew over the Cuckoo's Nest*. New York: Penguin, 2003.

Lencek, Lena, and Gideon Bosker. *Making Waves: Swimsuits and the Undressing of America*. San Francisco: Chronicle Books, 1989.

Le Zotte, Jennifer. "How the Summer of Atomic Bomb Testing Turned the Bikini into a Phenomenon." Smithsonian.com, May 21, 2015. http://www.smithsonianmag.com/smithsonian-institution/how-wake-testing-atomic-bomb-bikini-became-thing-180955346/.

Marx, Karl, and Friedrich Engels. "Manifesto of the Communist Party." In *The Marx and Engels Reader*, edited by Robert C. Tucker, 469–500. New York: W. W. Norton, 1978.

Masco, Joseph. *Nuclear Borderlands: The Manhattan Project in Post–Cold War New Mexico.* Princeton, NJ: Princeton University Press, 2006.

McCarthy, Cormac. *The Road.* New York: Vintage, 2006.

Mills, C. Wright. *Letters and Autobiographical Writings.* Edited by Kathryn Mills. Berkeley: University of California Press, 2001.

———. *Listen Yankee: The Revolution in Cuba.* New York: Ballantine Books, 1961.

———. *The Sociological Imagination.* New York: Oxford University Press, 1959.

———. "Sociological Poetry." *politics* (Spring 1948): 125–126.

———. *White Collar.* New York: Oxford University Press, 1951.

Moten, Fred. "Manic Depression: A Poetics of Hesitant Sociology." Lecture at The Centre for Comparative Literature, University of Toronto, April 4, 2017.

O'Neil, Robyn. "Prologue: The War against Fossils." In *Making Sense*, a brochure for the art show of the same name at the University of South Florida Contemporary Art Museum, Tampa, Florida, September 26–December 12, 2014, 5.

Phillips, Carl. "Dirt Being Dirt." *Poem-a-Day.* The Academy of American Poets, April 6, 2017, https://www.poets.org/poetsorg/poem/dirt-being-dirt.

Polenberg, Richard, ed. *In the Matter of J. Robert Oppenheimer: The Security Clearance Hearing.* Ithaca, NY: Cornell University Press, 2002.

Proust, Marcel. *Finding Time Again.* Translated by Ian Patterson. Vol. 6 of *In Search of Lost Time*, edited by Christopher Prendergast. New York: Penguin, 2003.

———. *The Fugitive.* Translated by Peter Collier. Vol. 5 of *In Search of Lost Time*, edited by Christopher Prendergast, 387–658. New York: Penguin, 2002.

———. *The Prisoner.* Translated by Carol Clark. Vol. 5 of *In Search of Lost Time*, edited by Christopher Prendergast, 3–384. New York: Penguin, 2002.

———. *Swann's Way.* Translated by Lydia Davis. Vol. 1 of *In Search of Lost Time*, edited by Christopher Prendergast. New York: Penguin, 2002.

Rubik, Ernő. Interview by Dave Simpson. *The Guardian*, May 26, 2015. https://www.theguardian.com/culture/2015/may/26/erno-rubik-how-we-made-rubiks-cube.

Sandburg, Carl. "Wilderness." In *The Complete Poems of Carl Sandburg*, 100. New York: Harcourt, 2003.

Sontag, Susan. "Notes on 'Camp.'" In *Against Interpretation and Other Essays*, 275–292. London: Penguin, 2009.

Speier, Hans. "Magic Geography." *Social Research* 8, no. 3 (1941): 310–330.

Spiegelman, Art. *Maus I: A Survivor's Tale; My Father Bleeds History.* New York: Pantheon, 1986.

Stewart, Kathleen. "Precarity's Forms." *Cultural Anthropology* 27, no. 3 (2012): 518–525.

Summers, John. "James Agee and C. Wright Mills: Sociological Poetry." In *Agee Agonistes: Essays on the Life, Legend, and Works of James*

Agee, edited by Michael A. Lofaro, 199–216. Knoxville: University of Tennessee Press, 2007.

Tarde, Gabriel. *Underground Man*. London: Duckworth, 1905.

Taussig, Michael. *The Nervous System*. New York: Routledge, 1992.

"This Day in History: July 5." History.com. http://www.history.com/this-day-in-history/bikini-introduced.

Turkina, Olesya. *Soviet Space Dogs*. London: Fuel, 2014.

Vanderbilt, Tom. *Survival City: Adventures among the Ruins of Atomic America*. Princeton, NJ: Princeton University Press, 2002.

Williams, Raymond. "Structures of Feeling." In *Marxism and Literature*, 128–135. New York: Oxford University Press, 1977.

Wolfe, Thomas. *Look Homeward, Angel*. New York: Scribner, 2006.

Wray, Matt. "A Blast from the Past: Preserving and Interpreting the Atomic Age." *American Quarterly* 58 (2006): 467–483.

ILLUSTRATIONS

print; 16 x 20 in. (40.64 x 50.8 cm). San Francisco Museum of Modern Art, Gift of The Estate of Gordon Matta-Clark. © Estate of Gordon Matta-Clark / SODRAC (2018). Photograph: Don Ross.

page 76. Statue of the Virgin Mary at St. Mary's Catholic Church in Oak Ridge. Photo by Linda Davidson. The Washington Post / Getty Images.

page 79. Photograph of American physicist J. Robert Oppenheimer, 1958. © Philippe Halsman / Magnum Photos.

page 82. Bob Ross, *A Mild Winter's Day*, season 17, episode 6. ®Bob Ross name and images are registered trademarks of Bob Ross Inc. © Bob Ross Inc. All rights reserved. Used with permission.

page 86. Neutron-irradiated dime. Personal collection of the author.

page 89 top. Atomic courier Frank McLemore as Athena, March 1968. Family photo.

page 89 bottom. AEC truck in the American landscape, April 1968. Family photo.

page 91. Nan McLemore with fox pelt, June 1968. Family photo.

page 96. First Cube Prototype 1 (wooden). Photograph courtesy of Liberty Science Center. Rubik's Cube® used by permission from Rubik's Brand Ltd. www.rubiks.com.

page 97. My cousin Gloria Haynes Brown in Halloween costume, 1983. Family photo.

page 101. *The Far Side* cartoon depicting bugs dancing gleefully as mushroom clouds explode in the background. Gary Larson, The Far Side®.

page 102. Cinnamon-flavored Atomic Fire Balls.

page 105. Topps® Garbage Pail Kids card used courtesy of The Topps Company, Inc. Image courtesy of the Browne Popular Culture Library, University Libraries, Bowling Green State University.

Writer and sociology professor Lindsey A. Freeman
is the author of *Longing for the Bomb: Oak Ridge
and Atomic Nostalgia* (2015).